THREE BRIDGES

ADULTHOOD IS EASY UNTIL LIFE INTERVENES

ANDREW S. KANE, OBE, PH.D.

Karen

Thank you for all of
your support & friendship.
It's meaning ful to me,
Enjoy the book.

Andy 12/18.

CONTENTS

"No one can build you the bridge on which you, and only you, must cross the river of life. There may be countless trails and bridges and demigods who would gladly carry you across: but only at the price of pawning and forgoing yourself. There is one path in the world that no one can walk but you. Where does it lead? Don't ask, walk!" —Nietzsche

ACKNOWLEDGMENTS

I am fortunate to have had many mentors in my life. I hope and trust that you know who you are and know that I am deeply grateful to you. You all have been an important part of my life. I am the fortunate one and indebted to those who have helped to shape and counsel me for better or worse, into the person I am today.

To those who have supported my journey in undertaking and completing my masters and doctorate degrees - thank you for intellectually motivating me and emotionally providing encouragement and support.

I want to thank Christie Hind who has been a strong supporter and advisor on my book. Thanks also to Margery Walshaw for her involvement in reviewing and editing my book.

To Chancellor Irv Katz and Academic Dean Inula Katz from the International University of Professional Studies, your encouragement and support as well as feeling your love in designing and completing both my masters and doctorate degrees will always be remembered. To psychologist, author, and coach Lloyd Thomas, who served as a mentor throughout my degrees, your insight, camaraderie, and support was invaluable.

To my many friends, including those who I interviewed during my doctoral thesis and those who have always spurned me on to write my book - simply said, thank you for being there and in my life. True friends are few rather than many, and those of you who we mutually feel ourselves as friends, you are priceless to me.

My deepest debt of gratitude goes to my family. The day my two "Gen X" boys, Brad and Nick, heard I was "going back to school" they insisted on buying me ice cream and a new backpack to encourage me to relive my college days - I only wish I could. The support of my entire immediate family has been constant and loving.

To my mother, still rocking as she approaches her nineties, Nick, Brad, my daughter-in-law Gena, my brother, Petyr, and my grand-daughter, Ayla, you all are so important in my life, each in your own way and I hope that you know this each time we hug and kiss each other. My father and grandparents passed away decades ago, but they have never left my heart, so they too are part of my inspiration and have helped shape me. In some respects, my life has been lived for the life I know my father wished he could have lived and if he senses this, wherever he is, then I hope I have given him something meaningful back for the support my parents gave me.

To my wife, Sarah, you are my rock, my closest friend, and you know it is true when we say we are made for each other. I am so lucky that we are true partners in life and in our journey, which has never been smooth, but which always has had a soft landing in your arms and heart. I deeply love my family - all of you.

From the day I wrote the first words of my doctoral dissertation to the day I completed this book, I decided that my book would be dedi-cated to my daughter, Kate, who left us way too early and is missed by so many. Every day I feel her love and can sense the half empty Coca Cola cans she would always leave in my study. I would often write my book in my pajamas just as she would wear them as her uniform at home.

I have learnt that life isn't easy, but neither is anything worth achieving. My daughter never survived long enough, merely 27 years, to enjoy and flourish in her life. To her, I dedicate my book and she will always have my unconditional love and a permanent place in my heart, like the rest of my family.

INTRODUCTION

Everyone has I suspect, certain expectations of what their life may be like and how it will unfold. Yet, if there is one certainty I have come to realize, it is that life does not always go according to plan. I have experienced and understood this firsthand.

In 1974 after graduating from University in England, I joined Arthur Andersen. Back then, most of the technological wonders that are commonplace today such as cell phones and the "cloud" did not exist as every day tools. I grew up with my grandparents who would recall the early days when cars, planes, and TVs were uncommon or not even around. Now, I recall in a similar fashion how just under 50 years ago life was so different. Indeed, change is the constant in our lives and how we handle it and the potential adversity that results with change, can test our resilience and shape our lives.

When I graduated from University, nobody handed me or anyone else for that matter, a manual that taught or prepared me for adult responsibilities such as being a husband, father, business colleague or how to juggle career aspirations with everyday life. I had extensive and incredible training at Arthur Andersen; it was focused on values such as stewardship or the motto, "Think Straight - Talk Straight." These are still great values, but I had to find my own way of navigating adulthood. There were times when I felt my work and personal life were out of balance with the challenges I faced of being a husband, father or colleague. Along the way, I had to address the stress of Arthur Andersen's collapse and the death of my daughter, as I navigated my way through adulthood.

After my daughter, Kate, died, I was personally motivated to understand adulthood far better, which is why I pursued my masters and doctorate degrees in Human Development. In this personal quest I paid particular attention to midlife since I was in its midst. I reflected on my own life experiences and focused on utilizing my masters and doctoral studies to take a broader view of adulthood.

It was during my doctoral research, and in particular, my PhD thesis on midlife, that I conceptualized adulthood as comprising three metaphorical bridges that we traverse as we move through adulthood.

These three metaphorical bridges generally correspond to ages 20-40, 40-60, and adulthood after age 60, but they should not be viewed as specifically age-related, but rather, stage based. I have termed these three bridges as:

1. *The Bridge of Accumulating Responsibilities;*
2. *The Midlife Bridge; and,*
3. *The Bridge of Decumulation and Simplicity*

I linked the journey of adulthood across these three bridges as to why and how it is important to enhance your wellbeing by embracing positive psychology so you can thrive as an adult, regardless of the stage of adulthood you are in.

As for me, once I had graduated in 1974 from the London School of Economics, part of the University of London, I was on a constant upward climb, striving and competing for promotions within my chosen profession at Arthur Andersen. I was immersed in extensive travel while wining, dining, and serving actual and potential clients. This no doubt all helped propel my career forward. I undertook all of this both first in London and then later, in Los Angeles, when I emigrated there with my then wife and baby son in 1978.

Yet, my personal life suffered due to my focus on my career.

Frankly, looking back I really did not understand in my twenties and thirties the true meaning of happiness. I felt like a plane in turbulent skies, buffeted around, missing my young children and growing family. Does this strike a chord in someone you know? I was surely not alone in a misplaced focus at this stage of my adult life. Eventually, I paid the heavy price when I ended up divorced in my late thirties. This was painful and it impacted not just me, but my children and my career. I needed to be resilient and learn how to deal with this unplanned change of events over time.

Looking back, my twenties and thirties were a time when I was "accumulating." This is why I coined the first bridge in adulthood as the Bridge of Accumulating Responsibilities. Not only did I accumulate promotions (or a lack of them), but I accumulated the responsibilities of being a spouse and father as well as accumulating assets and liabilities such as a house, cars and a mortgage that all come along to many of us in our twenties and thirties. Looking back, I was likely so consumed in creating my identity as a professional in my career that I failed to focus enough attention on being authentic in my self-identity and the need for work/life balance in this early stage of adulthood. I had lost a sense of my true self while hidden behind the mask of becoming a successful professional service provider.

My personal situation is, I suspect, not uncommon among many professionals such as lawyers and accountants. In an effort to combat this dilemma, many workplaces today offer flex time, remote work environments, maternity as well as paternity leave, increased vacation time, and sabbaticals. However, when toiling in the cauldron of a career, the pressure to succeed is plentiful. This may be defined as title, power, and the capacity to accumulate money. Thus, while technological advances may change and usher in new technologies and associated tools, the challenges we face in adulthood haven't really changed or lessened. They are simply recast in different ways, as society changes and decades roll by.

To illustrate, as the speed and expectations of communications has changed dramatically over the past few decades, having time to respond has shrunk. The instant access of mobile phones, the 24/7 presence of social media, and the ability to communicate with people anytime and anywhere creates additional stress for some. While progress brings about change, no doubt most good with perhaps some bad, how we adapt to change is important. We need to possess the skills required to adapt. Thus, our resilience has become increasingly important because a failure to adapt will certainly bring about additional stress.

Today, many people may observe that Millennials and Generation Z use Snapchat with ease, but Generation Xers may not have adapted as easily while Baby Boomers are even less likely to use Snapchat.

My view is that perhaps the challenges that some face today are no less than those experienced by earlier generations. In the 1970s and 1980s everything seemed to occur at a faster pace than that which occurred in the 1950s and 1960s. Thirty to forty years ago, we had the advent of fax machines, pagers, and early versions of computers. Today, the speed of communication is markedly faster than, the perceived fast speed of the '70s and '80s. This speed has been accentuated by social media. Millennials and Generation Z excel at social media and Baby Boomers (at least some, if they are willing to admit) may struggle at times. And yet, those same Baby Boomers were early adopters of their new technologies some 30 to 40 years ago. We may live in different times, but the changes we all experience, some of which I have described, can cause similar types of stress and demands on our adulthood and these stresses often increase as we enter midlife and mid-stage of our careers. A substantive life event can be so impactful on one's life and can result in significant change occurring. Often a life event can be abrupt or unexpected. It can be a challenge to our self-identity, and a substantive test on our resilience.

As for me, back in 2002, the unexpected happened when the prestigious Chicago-based, but truly worldwide professional services firm of Arthur Andersen, once considered part of the "Big Five" accounting firms, collapsed. The actions taken by the U.S. Government against Andersen, namely a Department of Justice injunction, caused Andersen's immediate downfall and 85,000 people lost their careers within weeks. Although the U.S. Supreme Court later overturned the actions taken by the Department of Justice, it was too late. The aftermath was a traumatic and emotional life event affecting professionals across the globe, and of course, their families, including mine.

I am sure that when Arthur Andersen collapsed in 2002 I was not the only one to ask a deep and personal question: "What's next?" My self-reflection back then, just as I approached my 50th birthday, was candidly focused on replacing lost income and capital. Looking back, my approach to answering "what's next" was not based on what would I be happy doing, but rather, how I could make up for the financial loss that I suffered?

Having spent almost 30 years with Arthur Andersen, I had developed a sense of permanence and a place that felt like home. Naturally, it would be difficult to move to a new environment that would come with a different set of values, culture, colleagues, and issues. Andersen's collapse was truly a life event for me and it certainly triggered emotions, a self-introspection, and played on my state of mind. When the shock of the unexpected loss from Arthur Andersen's collapse occurred, it provided me little time for thoughtful, long-term planning.

I probably could and should have probed my introspection more deeply. Unfortunately, this realization and my second introspection would not come for six years. Looking back, I now see that my efforts to reinvent myself in 2002 was not a complete success since I was only successful at relaunching and reinventing myself from a financial standpoint. As individuals, we all react differently when it comes to how life events trigger our reactions and responses.

The lesson I learnt in 2002 was a need for a deeper and more thoughtful introspection if another life event struck me. Unfortunately, such a life event did strike again when unfortunately, my daughter died in 2008 from liver cancer. I was now in my mid-fifties, certainly well into midlife. This loss shook me to my very core.

Kate passed away at only 27. I remember the day as it is burnt permanently into my brain. July 18, 2008. Not an ordinary day; indeed, by far the worst day of my life.

I started the day very early that morning going with my wife to the UCLA Medical Center where my daughter, who was critically ill and was scheduled to have a liver transplant that morning. There she lay on the gurney, ready for the operation. I kissed her skin, cool due to her being comatose, and I was then dispatched by the attendant nurses to wait in Maddie's Room, where families of patients wait until news of the operation is provided.

"Don't expect to see me for several hours," said the lead doctor who had called me the night before to let me know that a transplant liver was available. "If you see me before 11 a.m., it will not be good." I saw him just an hour or so later around 9:30 a.m. I had read in my head his words he was about to say when he pronounced that her abdomen was full of cancer and advised that a transplant was not possible. My heart shot through my stomach to the floor — the proverbial wind knocked out of the sails of not just myself, but my family. Reeling, I was asked to make the decision of whether to awaken her with the morbid news that she cannot have a transplant or have mercy on her and let her pass that day. To me, it was the worst decision a parent can make. I chose the humane answer. I could not bear to see her know her fate. Kate passed away that afternoon.

A few tragic hours later, I drove away from the UCLA Medical Center, the necessary paperwork duly signed. I headed up Beverly Glen, one of those winding and quaint Los Angeles canyons towards our then home on Mulholland Highway. It was while driving up the canyon, the late afternoon sun pouring into my car that I looked toward the heavens, while stationary at a traffic light and pondered again the same question from 2002, "What's next?"

My first reaction was that I still had no answer that I was comfortable with. I realized then that back in 2002 I had sidestepped that probing question only for it to come flooding back to me six years later. This time, I decided not to ignore it any longer. There and then I vowed to myself to take the time, effort, and research to find the right answer for me to "what's next?"

My daughter's death more than jolted me. It caused me to take a deep and hard look at my life, my lifestyle, my health, and my happiness. In one word, my wellbeing. Kate's death launched a journey for me in which I truly began to understand and recognize not only my own mortality, but also what I wanted to do with my life. I commenced a more authentic reinvention and to understand my true self, during the prime of my midlife.

No one had prepared me, nor as is likely the case for many, for the impact of midlife. Kate's death was my life event that triggered me to undertake my masters and doctorate degrees in Human Development t?hand my PhD thesis, which focused on addressing and overcoming midlife challenges.

Since 2008, I have been on my thoughtful journey. Through research undertook while completing my doctoral thesis, I came to understand and embrace the science of positive psychology and how, by applying the science, one can enhance one's own wellbeing and why this is important. During my doctoral research, I expanded my thinking and approach to solving midlife challenges by addressing the journey we each take through our adulthood. I discovered an area that I am passionate about (human development) and how I can share my insights, experience and knowledge in helping others. Through my research, I conceptualized and created the concept of three metaphorical bridges we traverse in adulthood, and how midlife fits into our journey through adulthood.

My book is designed to give back what I have learnt and experienced in my adulthood and help others navigate their lives, especially during midlife. Now, almost ten years after my daughter's death, I hope my book may help others think about how to successfully navigate their adulthood, traverse my three metaphoric bridges, and enhance their wellbeing.

ONE

ADULTHOOD AND THE THREE BRIDGES: AN OVERVIEW

E veryone would agree that being able to see into the future would be highly beneficial aside from no doubt being very lucrative. Imagine how helpful it would be when you can look back to see where you have come from and know where you should be headed.

Maybe, in a moment of sheer fantasy, I imagine if I could have peered ahead to my future life when I was in my twenties...perhaps my unbridled enthusiasm for the future may have been tempered by the reality of what was to come. Fortunately, I did not know what was to come!

The fact is, looking back has its benefits, even if we cannot look forward. Looking back and reflecting has enabled me to view adulthood as comprising an early, mid, and late stage, each of which varies in length for each person. I describe these stages as the three metaphorical bridges we cross in adulthood.

How many of us were handed a set of instructions on what, how, and when to behave in adulthood? None of us. Our parents, we hope, may have read a book about raising children, but as children, I suspect we didn't have access to a book for our own development. We did have our parents to educate and raise us, help us establish our values and morals, align our behaviors, and no doubt, they tried to shape us through their eyes.

As we graduate college and start out in the workforce, adulthood can and often does feel like an open pasture to wander around in — a blank canvas to paint our life as an adult. To some, this is thrilling, but to others it is scary and uncertain. However, as we start our travels through adulthood, one thing is certain: our uniqueness. We each come with our own set of values, traits, strengths, and personality that results in a journey that is unique and there to be enjoyed.

Adulthood represents 75% to 80% of our life span, which is a long period of time when we have far less guidance and shoulders to lean upon than in childhood.

The Three Metaphorical Bridges

I have conceptualized that we navigate three successive bridges that loosely represent the early, mid, and late stages of adulthood.

As previously mentioned, these three stages of adulthood are conceptualized as the Bridge of Accumulating Responsibilities, followed by the Midlife Bridge, and then lastly, the Bridge of Decumulation and Simplicity.

Navigating each bridge requires us to crystallize our understanding of where we are in each stage of our life. We must realize why the successful crossing of our present bridge is crucial to arrive at the next one and in the bigger picture see and understand the perspective of each stage of adulthood. This perspective can then be used to eventually understand the importance of revealing one's true self and why we need to thrive.

Positive Psychology

The science of positive psychology has twenty plus years of research in this area and demonstrated the proven benefits of enhancing one's wellbeing.

These proven benefits from the science of positive psychology are so powerful, that the pursuit of one's wellbeing should be a lifetime quest. Thus, the better equipped you are to thrive, the more successful the navigation of each metaphorical bridge of adulthood will be and the more likely you are to reap the proven benefits from enhancing your wellbeing.

Clearly, each stage of adulthood has its own set of challenges, yet there are several common challenges that are relevant to each bridge. One such challenge, as an illustration, is that despite one's best intentions and aspirations, life events will occur that will throw a wrench into your plans.

Life Events

These life events may include death, divorce, a health scare or job loss. Such life events can trigger within us an introspection of one's life. Simply through getting older, we move along in our life journey, yet I maintain that it is not just about making it across each bridge that is important, but how we enjoy the journey while undertaking it.

Happiness

If someone sets a goal to be happy, it should not be a goal to achieve at the end of one's journey, but rather, happiness should reside during the journey itself. There are many learned writings on this subject, but if you are not inclined to read centuries of script on this, my suggestion is to just ask people you respect who have lived a full and happy life whether all the sweat and toil is worth the result at the end of the day or if savoring each day along the journey is the better way to live?

Happiness is not an asset you can buy or something that can be rewarded as a retirement gift; it is a state of being that you personally experience throughout life.

How many of us can recall back to the early years of our adulthood when we graduated college with brimming expectations of finding the career of our dreams, meeting our one true love, and living a happy and successful life both personally and professionally? These are indeed highly obtainable goals, but they are not achieved without a high degree of uncertainty about when and if our aspirations can be realized.

Aspirations

When our aspirations and hopes fail to materialize, this in itself can be a challenge, especially when the evaporation of a dream occurs in midlife. One example is that as time unfolds, our careers may not experience the rapid, upward climb that we had hoped for when we were still fresh-faced and full of optimism upon leaving university. Another example is when we find love only to learn that it isn't everlasting, and sometimes marriage ends in divorce. Our aspirations may not materialize, challenging us to accept the "intrapersonal challenge" of dreams tempered by reality.

Life Challenges

Achieving our own aspirations is but one of three challenges we face as our life unfolds. A second challenge in adulthood is that we all age and there comes that day when you notice you have white hairs, or your injuries do not heal as quickly as before, or your physique is no longer youthful. These are "physiological challenges" we will need to address during adulthood.

We also have to face "interpersonal challenges" as we move into our forties and fifties. Balancing a career with raising a family and the demands of nurturing a marriage and raising children poses new responsibilities and sometimes unexpected pressures of dealing with other people as they mature.

Stages of Adulthood

Adulthood for most of us is not a piece of cake. It is not easy to know how one can or why indeed one should thrive. I realize that this may sound simplistic, but without a book of instructions (since one has never existed), the journey of life is unpredictable and fraught with challenges interspersed with celebrations of joy. What I have observed is that as we cannot control the future or others. However, we can take control of our self and ask and seek how authentic we want to be, what relationships we desire, what emotions we wish to feel, express, and manage, what accomplishments we want to strive for, what provides us a sense of purpose, how present we want to be with others, and how we can strive to be healthy. These are components that assist us to thrive.

My three metaphorical bridges symbolize our progress from the first stage of adulthood, that of youthful adulthood, through midlife to a latter period of adulthood. Midlife is the second stage of adulthood and is sandwiched between the first and last stage of adulthood, and as will be explained later, should be viewed as the opportunity to explore and redefine oneself to enjoy what is often referred to as the second half of life.

The third stage of adulthood is often the time when we are focused on the notion of or actually enjoying what has traditionally been known as retirement. However, with increased longevity during this third stage of adulthood is perhaps the time when your career has peaked, and you feel the need for change for a second act. This is where encore careers play an important role for many who "retire" from a job or career they have been invested in for many decades.

Retirement, Rewirement and Reinvention

From my perspective, "retirement" is the wrong terminology to apply to many people as I like to think that since we are living longer, we should shun the use of the word retirement and in its place, focus on "rewirement" in order to reinvent oneself during our fifties, sixties, and beyond.

Recognizing that at a certain age one may "retire" from a career, but still feel passion, drive and the ability to be productive, this state of mind and being often permits people to pursue their true passions by rewiring how they think, believe, and behave in a lifestyle of choice.

Reinvention is, in my mind, about seeking a happier lifestyle of choice. As we travel throughout our adulthood, it is likely that there will be a time when we will ponder questions and internally reflect about:

- *What really matters in my life?*
- *What makes me truly and constantly happy?*
- *Can I find peace of mind?*
- *How should I treat others?*
- *What makes for great relationships?*
- *Can I be happier in my career?*
- *Should society care about happiness?*
- *How can we create a happier world?*

Personally, my daughter's death impacted me profoundly. It was the most devastating event of my life. It challenged me to seek and achieve a deeper self-introspection. So, when I asked myself for the second time after my daughter died "what's next," I realized that the answer for me, required a deeper self-introspection. This journey has led me through my doctoral research to explore adulthood, especially midlife challenges and how a reinvention coupled with applying the science of positive psychology can enhance your wellbeing and provide enduring happiness. After all, isn't this what we all want?

Spirituality

As we travel through adulthood, we are likely to come to a place and time in our life when we have a greater interest in being our true self, have a desire to pursue our passions, and likely have an interest to address our own mortality, and for some, seek more spirituality in our life.

Spirituality should not be confused with religion. It is an embracing force that encompasses the development of a sense of purpose, altruism, and is also important in addressing and accepting our own mortality. This is especially true during midlife when we may contemplate a need to rewire or reinvent as a result of a self-introspection, often triggered by a life event. Spirituality can be thought of as an increased emphasis on how we experience ourselves in the world.

"Vertical spirituality" describes a desire to transcend one's individual ego while "horizontal spirituality" is a desire to be of service to other humans and the planet. We should view a pursuit of spirituality as an on-going journey characterized by an intense, consuming motivation to "become," by which we seek transformative experiences of ourselves and the world. Many become more spiritual as a way to create a sense of purpose or meaning in one's life as well as those around us. This is an important part of addressing midlife and an important element in positive psychology and how to increase your own wellbeing.

Concluding Reflections

The three stages of adulthood I have described above are not specifically age based. Rather, they result from natural transitions, and are therefore, stage based. Some people experience a smooth journey across all their metaphorical bridges while for others it can be daunting. Just as change is easy for some people to accept and adapt to, while for others it is frightening.

Change may sometimes need to be addressed because events force change, such as a job loss, health issues, divorce, etc. However, there are occasions when the change is driven within. For example, to pursue a career or vocation that you enjoy. Life events can be a pathway to change and are like a shock to your system. They can occur at any age and stage of life. As we age, we are more likely to find that substantive life events trigger ourselves to question how we have conducted our life. Often, we seek to make changes and most importantly, why we need to make a change in our life. One of the reasons we seek a deeper introspection is because we have aged. While in our twenties and/or thirties, we are normally forward looking – building a career, family, etc. At this stage of our adulthood, we are not likely thinking about our mortality. Rather, we have the open road ahead, full of dreams and opportunities. It is when we face challenges, such as those that are physiological, intrapersonal, and interpersonal in nature that we think deeper about our life.

I have known too many professionals who went into law or

accounting after university, but who never really had a passion for service and really desired within themselves to do something different or be someone else. This disillusionment and the internal desire to be more authentic and reveal one's true self often manifests itself during the crossing of the midlife bridge.

It is only as we age and have accumulated assets and liabilities, including developing relationships with the most important people in our lives, such as a spouse and children, that we start to see the time horizon of our life and obtain additional clarity to our values. Indeed, life events are not just shocks, but they can force us to see the road ahead as not necessarily being wide open. As we age, our ability to understand our time horizon and our own mortality becomes clearer and this, in turn, impacts how we address our own mortality during adulthood.

No doubt every one of us knows someone who has experienced a major setback in their life. Ask yourself whether your empathy for their plight is overshadowed by the respect and awe you may have for how they have addressed their challenge and overcome it by their resilience? These are often our heroes who have displayed courage as well as resilience. Our capacity to bounce back is an important part of building character, just as is the courage to make changes and address issues.

When we have role models, coaches, and mentors to help guide us through our challenges, we are clearly better off, but our own internal compass is important too. Having a sense of one's values, understanding one's strengths, managing one's emotions and following your moral compass are all important. They are all important to help overcome life challenges, address issues, align one to have clarity of what one is passionate about, and most importantly, clarify what provides one with a sense of meaning or purpose. These are all relevant to our wellbeing.

TWO

YOUR WELLBEING AND THE SCIENCE OF POSITIVE PSYCHOLOGY

B efore we meander, saunter, walk, run, or sprint through our adulthood, we ought to reflect how important it is to be constantly happy, or what the scientists refer to as enhancing your wellbeing. This latter topic is at the heart of the science of positive psychology with a focus on how and why people thrive. If you ever ask someone what they want most out of life, happiness is usually close, if not at the top of the list.

A Historical Perspective of Happiness

From a historical perspective, the concept of happiness has been studied for thousands of years by great thinkers dating back to Ancient Greece and in particular Aristotle, who wrote in 350 BC in his *Nicomachean Ethics* about the good life for the individual and the community by living a moral and virtuous existence.

In the late 1990s, the psychologist Martin Seligman, then president of the American Psychological Association, noted that the clear majority of psychology was focused on mental illness rather than mental health. Another pioneer of positive psychology Mihaly Csikszentmihalyi, a pre-eminent social psychologist, became interested in the concept of resiliency and the psychology of optimal experience.

Even religious texts and spiritual leaders have emphasized the benefits of "positivity," what many refer to as good living and positive character. Western monotheistic religions suggest that certain personal virtues such as forgiveness, self-sacrifice, faith, and loyalty are valuable attributes and likely to lead to success in the world. Whether it be philosophy, religion, or humanistic psychology (such as that put forward by Abraham Maslow), there is a basic assumption that people are capable of goodness and can become better. All of this has created the path that led to the focus and research around positive psychology.

What differentiates positive psychology from earlier approaches is its careful, empirical research. In studying this science, I found that positive psychology and the ensuing benefits gained from enhancing one's wellbeing is highly relevant in both developing your career and enriching your life.

The early days of positive psychology involved scientists studying various topics such as hope, happiness, creativity, and gratitude. Martin Seligman brought the pioneers of this science together. In his book, "*Character Strengths and Virtues: A Handbook and Classification,*" Seligman wrote about the exercising of signature strengths to add an element of authenticity and to raise the quality of happiness to a higher level. This book identified six core virtues and 24 human strengths that provide the routes to achieving these core virtues.

According to Martin Seligman, signature strengths also play a key role in enhancing the quality of one's life. His research led to the identification and development of the qualities that can best help a person to maximize wellbeing and buffer against life's difficulties. Positive relationships are one of the core elements in how positive psychology is constructed with character strengths being a key pathway to creating stronger, deeper connections. Character strengths help to recognize and amplify what is positive rather than focus on what is challenging or wrong with a person.

I believe that to thrive, understanding and playing to your strengths is important. When I coach, I help clients to understand their strengths. There are multiple strength assessment tools available.

When you can understand and relate to your strengths, such as which ones energize rather than drain you, then you can focus on these positive strengths and apply them. Hopefully, to enhance your personal life, career, or both.

As early as 1990, Mihaly Csikszentmihalyi's book, *"Flow: The Psychology of Optimal Experience,"* established the positive side of being a human being, which the author termed as "flow." Mihaly Csikszentmihalyi also brought up the concepts of adaptation and resilience by questioning why some people with limited resources can weather life storms better than other people who have more resources.

Martin Seligman wrote in his book, *"Flourish: A Visionary New Understanding of Happiness and Wellbeing,"* about five core elements known as the PERMA theory of positive psychology. Since then, many researchers have added a sixth element — health. The acronym is known as PERMAH. We shall look at this in more depth later in this chapter.

The Focus of Positive Psychology

The focus of the science of positive psychology is to facilitate high human potential to help people become stronger, more productive, and happier. It is this evolution of thought and proven scientific research that underpins how I developed my own PhD dissertation about midlife and in turn, developed a professional coaching model utilizing the science of positive psychology to assist in mid-life reinvention.

Over the years, research has proven that when one applies the science of positive psychology, you can enhance your wellbeing and reap the benefits.

Subjective Wellbeing/Happiness and Factors Impacting It

From my perspective and in a somewhat simplistic fashion, I believe that happiness and subjective wellbeing can be interchanged as terminology when discussing the science of positive psychology.

Subjective wellbeing is the term used in public policy and the scientific name for how people evaluate their lives. Another way one can view subjective wellbeing is in terms of happiness and life satisfaction. This can be orientated into thinking and feeling that your life is going well, not badly.

Positive psychology is the science that underpins and validates the benefits that flow from an enhanced state of subjective wellbeing. This area has been researched widely over the past 20 years or so and the benefits proven, as will be explained in the next chapter of my book.

In time, we all come to understand that life will throw you challenges and life events will occur to each of us. Therefore, the level of one's wellbeing is naturally influenced by many internal, external, and psychological factors and thus, how you view your state of wellbeing may likely be subjective in nature.

- *Internal factors can be your outlook on life, your inborn temperament, your personality, and your resilience.*
- *External factors can include your levels of income and depths of relationships with friends, family, and your community.*
- *Psychological factors include our aspirations for our career and family, our social comparisons, and our ability to adapt to circumstances.*

Our happiness or one's subjective wellbeing is a process that results from these internal, external, and psychological factors which in turn, influences the way we behave. Happiness does not just feel good, but it is also good for colleagues, clients, family members, and others in the community around you.

If you have worked hard to significantly enhance your wellbeing it is not just about a pleasant outcome, but the effort and journey is an important factor in one's personal and professional success. Researchers have studied the outcomes of the state of one's subjective wellbeing and found that people who are happy are more likely to be healthier, live longer, and be more productive.

Simply put, if we can understand, accept, and embrace the fact that subjective wellbeing is important, and one works to enhance it, then research indicates you will be healthier and more productive.

Measuring Happiness/Subjective Wellbeing

Researchers have been quite adept at measuring happiness. These measurements have been based upon self-surveys and scales, particularly measuring life satisfaction, positive and negative feelings, and whether one is psychologically flourishing.

Over the past twenty years, there are three types of happiness that have often been analyzed — high life satisfaction, frequent positive feelings, and infrequent negative feelings. To expand and illustrate about measurements, it is beneficial to briefly look at each one:

A HIGH LIFE SATISFACTION -

This can be illustrated with statements such as "I think my life is great," or "I am satisfied with my job." In turn, by possessing this point of view, it can result in a more rewarding income, assist in achieving your goals, and help one have a higher self-esteem.

FREQUENT POSITIVE FEELINGS -

These feelings can be thought of when one is enjoying life and loving others, which in turn means you likely have supportive freedom or autonomy, probably have interesting work, and often an extroverted personality.

INFREQUENT NEGATIVE FEELINGS -

These feelings, with an emphasis on infrequent, could result in having fewer chronic worries or rarely feeling sad or angry, which in turn leads to lower levels of neuroticism, having harmony among your goals, and having a positive outlook on life.

It has been well written and researched that happiness really does not equate to the content of one's bank account or the value of one's stock portfolio. Without doubt, a minimum level of income is required to meet one's needs, but there is much more to happiness than wealth. In fact, research has shown that materialistic people are often less happy. Thus, investing in relationships and areas other than finances may be a prudent self-investment as it may show how well we can adapt and bounce back from change and adversity.

Adapting to Change and Resilience

I have personally found in my life that if one thing is constant, it is change. I suspect that this is true for many. There are always new experiences to face, enjoy, or conquer new relationships, colleagues, responsibilities, technologies, problems, issues, and challenges.

It is thus not surprising that one's level of subjective wellbeing is related to the process of adapting well to change and honing the skill of resilience in order to have the ability to bounce back when setbacks occur.

Adaptation is important in understanding the real notion of happiness. This is because if you experience a good or bad event, your initial reaction may be strong, such as being very happy or sad. However, over time one adapts to the event and you return to the former state of happiness before the event. For example, an evening out with friends may make you feel happy; however, after the evening is over, the experience passes as you adapt back to everyday life. Similarly, when devastating life events occur such as the death of a parent or a loss of a job, then the capacity to possess resilience enables you to bounce back to the original state of happiness before the loss.

The good news is that resilience is not only an important skill, but also a skill that can be learned such as when a person needs to know how to recover from negative events like being passed over for promotion. Thus, learning to become resilient is important to each person and requires that we invest in ourselves to learn how to adapt and become more resilient, in order to enhance our wellbeing.

The Science of Positive Psychology including PERMA

The focus of positive psychology is to look at what is right with people. Specifically, positive psychology is not a philosophy, but is a science that examines when people are at their best and flourishing.

However, I believe that it is important to understand that the science is not focused on the positive at the expense of the negative. Consequently, negative emotions or failures and losses are natural and important elements in our lives and play a role in our wellbeing.

The science provides an empirical burden of evidence with an emphasis on positive change and optimal functioning. Positive psychology is concerned with evidence, measurement, and testing where research results have created real world interventions focused on optimal performance. Although the science of positive psychology is only about twenty years old, it continues to be actively researched and tested. Yet, in many ways, its principles are not new concepts.

The six elements known by the acronym PERMAH have many subsets that have been tested, developed, and adopted by coaches, psychologists, and researchers. Topics like resilience, courage, how to manage emotions, one's grit or developing strengths are all relevant and related to these core elements. Let us look at each in more detail:

- *(P) Positive emotions, which is the right balance of heartfelt positivity to boost resilience.*
- *(E) Engagement, which is the regular development of our strengths, namely those things we are good at and enjoy doing.*
- *(R) Relationships, which is the creation of authentic, energizing connections.*
- *(M) Meaning, which is a sense of connection to something bigger than ourselves.*
- *(A) Accomplishment, which is the belief and ability to do the things that matter most to us.*
- *(H) Health, which is our vitality through eating well, moving regularly, sleeping deeply.*

Because positive psychology is a relatively new science, there are many opinions on the factors that contribute to enhancing one's wellbeing. My conclusion based upon my research and reading about the science, is to not be rigid with theories of wellbeing.

In fact, there are many excellent issues and topics that contribute to the science of positive psychology and much to be commended to read, focus on, and learn about. These include subjects such as authenticity, grit, humility, self-compassion, empathy, mindfulness, forgiveness, gratitude, self-acceptance, or emotional intelligence, as examples. Each of these topics has been worthy of books that explore each in depth. Suffice to say that the science of positive psychology is young, expanding, and flourishing.

I believe that one best practice is to help people develop during their adulthood an attitude to not be dogmatic, but rather, apply cutting edge research from the science of positive psychology to enhance their wellbeing in areas such as:

- *Building, sustaining, and deepening authentic relationships*
- *Honing personal/business development and communication skills*
- *Focus on managing emotions and developing positive ones*
- *Successfully navigating life transitions*
- *Understand and align one's values, strengths, and talents*

Each of the core elements of positive psychology are important. However, when they are all focused on and combined in practice, they can become powerful in enhancing your wellbeing.

Applying positive psychology is not a one size fits all approach, which is why I believe that as one matures as an adult your wellbeing should be customized to each person's individual needs. The benefits of applying the science of positive psychology have been well researched and documented. They include productivity improvement, more effective collaboration, the ability to generate more business and deeper friendships due to stronger relationships, and improving resilience to allow one to better handle stress. All of these benefits assists one's overall health and a sense of feeling happier.

The Impact of Neuroplasticity on Positive Psychology

I admit that it is probably easier to write about positive psychology than actually applying it to make changes in your life. Without a doubt, applying positive psychology can be hard work even when one knows that there are benefits worthy of the effort. So how do we initiate change? This is where the science of neuroplasticity comes in.

Research on neuroplasticity has shown that we can change regardless of age. However, I believe to change your behavior there must be a desire to make a change. A life event such as a health scare, death of a parent, or divorce can serve as a trigger for change. The adage, "I'm too old to change," is just not true. When someone states they don't want to change, such an attitude may exhibit a lack of a desire, courage, will, or motivation to change.

The science of neuroplasticity explains the way the brain acts and changes; and thus, neuroplasticity is critical in how to apply positive psychology.

Within the brain, neurons or synapses fire and wire together. The more we use this neural pathway, the more developed it becomes and the more developed the pathway, the more automatic it becomes. Thus, greater cognitive capacity will come from having more neurons or synapses, higher levels of neurogenesis (which is the creation of new neurons, especially in the memory-forming hippocampus within the brain), and increased production of compounds such as brain-derived neurotrophic factor (BDNF), which stimulates the production of neurons and synapses.

Together, the formation of neurogenesis and synapse increase learning, memory, reasoning, and creativity. Therefore, in people who excel at tasks, brain circuits tend to be more efficient with higher capacity and more flexibility by using less energy.

The brain also produces dopamine, which stimulates motivation. Motivation is considered good stress, such as the feeling you may have before taking an exam or preparing for a public speech. It is the flooding of dopamine that helps with memory and motivation. Conversely, bad stress is what we feel when we are under attack. The brain produces cortisol, which coats neurons and thus, impairs signal transmission and allows underlying abilities, such as to fight or flight, to reach their full potential.

The rule, "Neurons that fire together, wire together," suggests that a focus on mental training exercises regardless of age, should boost mental prowess.

Concluding Reflections

Neuroscientists believe that people can change regardless of age and therefore, people can reinvent at any stage, too.

Assuming one has the desire and motivation to want to change, positive psychology provides the evidence-based science for an individual to experience sustained happiness and an increased state of wellbeing, while the science of neuroplasticity explains how the brain works to cause the change in behavior and thinking required to make the change.

From a physiological standpoint, neuroplasticity can be viewed as our brain's ability to adapt in response to new situations or changes in one's environment. With the ability of the brain to adapt, neuroplasticity is a key link to successfully applying positive psychology to achieve desired benefits.

The power of our brain to rewire is the reason why we can learn new ways to behave and think, how we can improve our own resilience, how we manage our emotions, our approach to building and deepening relationships, or how we remain focused and engaged while we are at work or elsewhere. These are all important factors that contribute to enhancing our wellbeing.

Often as humans we utilize a carrot and stick theory to our lives. If deploying a stick is not wanting to remain unhappy or mitigate less than optimum health, then the carrot is the demonstrated benefit of an enhanced state of wellbeing, which we shall explore further in the next chapter.

THREE

HARNESSING THE BENEFITS FROM ENHANCING YOUR WELLBEING

Once you appreciate and understand the basics of the science of positive psychology, then the reason to enhance your subjective wellbeing is because you want to understand the payoff and strive to enjoy the benefits.

Fortunately, a lot of research has been conducted on both individuals and organizations. This research has proven that the following benefits can be experienced by enhancing your wellbeing:

- *Improved performance and productivity*
- *Better health and a longer life span*
- *Increased creativity and a faster thought process*
- *Greater caring, being more altruistic and more socially engaged*
- *Enhanced teaming and collaboration*
- *Faster career development*
- *Deeper relationships with family, friends, clients, and colleagues*
- *Sustained sense of engagement, presence, and focus*
- *Intensified empathy, gratitude, and compassion*
- *An aligned work/life balance through sustained happiness*

The Benefits of a Positive State of Mind

Some may consider happiness to be a whimsical notion since it may be viewed as difficult to quantify. Yet, subjective wellbeing is important because it is hard to imagine a good society in which people live in a desirable way, but are unhappy or dissatisfied. Wellbeing is subjective because how people feel about their lives is personal. As wellbeing can be measured in a meaningful and reliable way, so can happiness be measured.

The research on subjective wellbeing is well documented. The conclusion is that a sustainable, positive state of the human condition can enhance capability and functioning, improve social relationships, increase health and longevity as well as enable thriving communities. This positive state contrasts sharply with the downward spiral that is commonly seen in people who lead unhappy, unfulfilled, or material-istic lives.

The research demonstrates that there is a correlation among the factors that generate positive state of mind and they include:

1. *having satisfaction with life*
2. *having meaning and spirituality*
3. *possessing positive attitudes and emotions*
4. *having loving social relationships*
5. *having engaging activities and work*
6. *possessing values and life goals*

How the benefits can be impacted by the environment and culture you live in...

The environment in which a person is immersed in their life is also an important factor. Some environmental conditions have long lasting effects on one's wellbeing such as unemployment and poverty.

Culture will also make a difference to your state of wellbeing with some cultures having higher levels of subjective wellbeing. One reason is that in some cultures, happiness is valued more than in others. For example, the United States is an individualistic society, while many Asian countries are collective societies where the family is dominant, rather than the individual.

An illustration of the impact that culture can play is to note how we manage and express our emotions, which differs between individualistic and collective societies. The latter, collective societies, lean to passive and positive emotions while the former (individualistic societies) is related to active and positive emotions.

The Psychological Benefits of Enhancing Your Wellbeing

There are multiple psychological benefits from enhancing one's wellbeing. These benefits can include:

- *self-acceptance*
- *the establishment of quality ties to others*
- *a sense of autonomy in thought and action*
- *the ability to manage complex environments to suit personal needs and values*
- *the pursuit of meaningful goals and a sense of purpose in life*
- *continued growth and development as a person*

Increased Subjective Wellbeing and the Community

Subjective wellbeing has become a matter of national policy in many countries and now is measured in society, as documented in the World Happiness Report. The World Happiness Report is an annual publication of the United Nations Sustainable Development Solutions Network which contains rankings of national happiness and analysis of the data from various perspectives. The World Happiness Report is edited by John F. Helliwell, Richard Layard, and Jeffrey Sachs.

There are a wide range of community or societal benefits of enhancing wellbeing. It is to the benefit of society that happier people are more productive at work. Indeed, people who are happier as young adults have been found to earn more than their peers later in life. Furthermore, happier people have been proven to possess better relationships, make a positive contribution to society, and are less likely to engage in risky behavior. It is therefore evident that an enhanced state of wellbeing brings huge benefits to society and to your community when you focus on enhancing your wellbeing.

FOUR

ADULT DEVELOPMENT THEORY

As adults, we continue to develop as we age. Adult development theory is a lens to better understand dynamics between adults and shed a light on why adult relationships are sometimes not aligned at different stages of adult growth. When two people are in different stages of their adult development, they may have differing ways of communicating, possess divergent expectations, opinions, or values.

We transition as adults to higher stages of development and while our physical growth has ceased, our internal growth continues (i.e. our mental and intellectual growth). Adult development theory involves adults developing an independent sense of self and gaining traits associated with wisdom and social maturity while we also become more self-aware and increasingly capable to manage relationships and social situations.

Adult Development Theory

Our biological changes influence our psychological, interpersonal, and social developmental changes. These changes are often described by stage theories that focus on "age appropriate" developmental tasks to be achieved at each stage. Psychologists such as Erik Eriksen, Carl

Jung, Robert Kegan, Michel Common, and Daniel Levinson have each proposed stage theories of human development. These theories encompass the entire life span and more importantly, emphasize the potential for positive change very late in life.

One interesting adult development theory was developed by Dr. Robert Kegan. I believe it can be used to frame and understand parents and adult children in their stages of adult development. Dr Kegan postulated five stages of adult development. As these are outlined below, take note that about 65% of the general population never make it past stage three. In each stage, an adult can mature within a stage (lateral development) or mature into a higher stage (vertical development). These five stages are based upon two key concepts in adult development: transformation and subject-object shift.

Transformation can be thought of as how we view our world. What you may see as a child or as an adult looks completely different as we develop. Think of the emphasis, importance, or messaging we may receive when we were young adults versus when we are older. Examples may be how we reacted to the same movies we may have seen first as a young adult versus as an older adult, or how we view and use our own time line, or what is really important to us (e.g. health versus material assets). It is only through transformation that we transition to higher stages of development and why a personal tragedy (e.g. a life event), can be such a catalyst for our growth.

Subject-object shift involves knowing what we know from subject (where it is controlling us) to object (where we can control it). The more we consider an object, the more clearly, we see the world, ourselves, and the people around us. Think of this subject as "I am" and object as "I have". Subject (I am) are self-concepts that we are attached to and thus, we have no objectivity about. Object (I have) is when we are detached and we look at, reflect upon, engage in, exert control over, or connect to something else.

Dr. Kegan's five stages of adult development are:

- *Stage 1 - an impulse mind (early childhood)*
- *Stage 2 - an imperial mind (adolescence - about 6% of the adult population)*

- *Stage 3 - a socialized mind (58% of the adult population)*
- *Stage 4 - a self-authoring mind (35% of the adult population)*
- *Stage 5 - a self-transforming mind (1% of the adult population)*

Think of how you, your spouse, your siblings, parents, or your adult children (to the extent they are present in your life), fall into each stage. Likely, no one we know who is an adult, is at stage 1.

Stage 2 is akin to being an adolescent where the world surrounds you and is about meeting your own needs, interests, and agenda. Relationships are transactional, which are a way of achieving your own needs. Perceptions are important such as how others view you and the consequences that flow from their perceptions of you. Thus, if you are at stage two, you are more likely to follow rules. C heating does not occur because of the consequences of cheating, not because it goes against personal values, as they are less developed.

Stage three is where most of us fall. We are focused on interpersonal relationships, seeking mutuality of interest and external sources shape our self and our sense of the world. While in stage two the most important things are our personal needs and interests. In stage three, ideas, norms, and beliefs of people and systems around us are most important.

In reaching stage four, we are focused on self-authorship, identity, and ideology. We define ourselves by who we are and are not defined by other people or the environment. We can distinguish the thoughts and opinion of others and form our own. This stage is defined by being consumed with "who I am and what I stand for," with a developed sense of direction and the capacity to create and follow our own course.

Stage five is represented by only 1% of the general population, but represents a stage as an adult when we are exploring our own identities and roles. It represents the ever-changing self by interacting with others. We are not only questioning authority, but also questioning ourselves and are no longer held prisoner by our own identity, as we can hold multiple thoughts and ideologies at once.

As we progress through adulthood, our growth is not just about gaining new skills, status, or money. Within stages four and five, we are defining and reshaping ourselves (self-authoring), what we believe in, our intrapersonal sense of self and our interpersonal relationships with others, rather than accepting these from others. The key is to view the self as an object with a sense of detachment that can be evaluated, analyzed, and understood. As an aside, when we are in midlife, it is this self-introspection that promotes our growth in revealing and defining one's true self and the desire to be truly authentic.

Applying Adult Development Theory

When adult dynamics are not harmonious and conflict brews, it can be damaging. For example, a family not appearing to be on the same page and say working within a family-owned business can indicate dysfunctional management that is harmful to the business and possibly, the family as well. A parent may look at an issue one way while an adult child looks at the same issue completely differently. Their relationship is likely to be perceived by either the parent or child (or indeed others) to be that of a controlling boss/subordinate employee or a parent/still adolescent child. These dynamics can create significant conflict as the parent ages and adult children enter into their prime executive years.

Take for example Glenn Hoddle (not his real name), who is a highly successful first generation entrepreneur and has spent his whole adult life building Greaves Inc., a profitable family business. Glenn has always held the dream that his oldest son Harry, might one day take over the family business. After Harry returned home from college, Glenn assigned Harry around different divisions of Greaves Inc. to grow Harry's understanding of the business and groom him for the future day when Harry might replace him. Of late, Glenn has gotten cold feet, and recently confided:

"Harry just does not leave me with the impression that he looks like a CEO. I worry that he doesn't see the big picture and he is not aware of how people see him. I love him and am proud of him, but he is always trying to please others and is not yet his own man."

In the above example, son Harry has not yet reached stage three and may still be in stage two. Technically competent, Harry may not have developed or socialized to the point pf developing the level of independent thought and judgement that his father expects. His father, Glenn, is expecting Harry to be demonstrating attributes of stages three or four, and thus, unmet expectations causes Glenn, the dad, to question the readiness of Harry to step into his shoes as CEO of Greaves Inc. In turn, this erodes trust between them and can result in diminished expectations.

Many parents and adult children hold lingering doubts that the other will ever change. The good news is that we can change. As humans, we are wired to develop, grow, transform, and exceed one another's expectations. Many times, however, parents and adult children do not allow the "other" to grow or develop in their eyes. This short sightedness can lead to disappointment and conflict.

Here is another example. Danny (not his real name) is the father who has built the family owned business, Chivers Refrigeration. Danny has had a thorough "life" education after leaving school early while in his late teens and has enjoyed financial rewards through hard work, determination, and a tight control over the business. Likely the business is a reflection of Danny's identity. Danny could be an adult in stage two. Pattie, his daughter, who also works in the family business, has received the best academic education including an MBA, and has grown by the time of her thirties into stage three. In fact, her frequent travels around the world has permitted her to extensively experience many cultures and she may even be at stage four. Contrast this with her father, Danny, who never took a "gap" year, didn't travel until much later in his life, had started working while in his late teens, and thus, likely has a different outlook on life.

Danny and Pattie may have differing approaches to the family business as well as different perspectives, values, and priorities of life itself. Danny may see the world revolving around him, while Pattie is more detached in her outlook and likely has a greater sense of self. While sitting around the family dining table, the family dynamics may produce spirited conversation about politics, religion, and social issues with divergent views. However, this may translate and be interpreted within the family business as though the management or ownership team are not on the same page, displaying a lack of harmony and a lack of collaborative teaming. As Danny has not matured in his growth to stage three or beyond, he may find it hard to detach his relationship with Pattie and view the relationship objectively. He may see her still as his child not as an executive, while Pattie sees herself at Chivers Refrigeration as an executive. The result is that potential conflict can ensue.

Being able to objectively look at a relationship, issue, or scenario in a detached manner could perhaps help a parent see their adult child as a skilled and growing executive and treat them as such, with greater empowerment, responsibility, accountability, and trust. Unfortunately, this sometimes does not occur. The adult child wants to be treated as an executive, but is in their mind, still treated as a child. This breeds friction.

The good news is that we are never too old to learn how to change our behaviors and thoughts. The science of neuroplasticity has shown that we can train our brain. All of the adult development theories are clear on this point. So, the capacity to grow and move to a higher stage, is possible by cultivating curiosity, critical reflection, and openness. To grow, you also need to answer an important question, "What do I want?" Thinking through your answer to this question is important in order to gain clarity and a lack of ambiguity on what you want. Another relevant question to answer is to understand your motivations. Your growth can be assisted by making decisions (even small ones) that are aligned with your wants and values after answering these questions in a detached manner.

Concluding Reflections

Applying adult development theory as a broad development point of reference can provide both the empathy and understanding about how we all are at different stages of our development. The result of this awareness can reduce conflict and stress in the natural evolution and development of adult relationships. Moving through these stages of adult development is not linear. It is complex as this theory is really a road map to how adults develop.

The positive take away for adults is to use adult development theory to assist in being able to focus discussions, improve communi-cation, and trust. Often, resolving interpersonal conflicts are more about trying to understand versus trying to change. Using adult devel-opment theory can reduce negative feelings of judgement and criti-cism, and enhance understanding and acceptance of differences, such as what I care about, and what you care about.

FIVE

THE BRIDGE OF ACCUMULATING RESPONSIBILITIES

The first metaphorical bridge in adulthood is the Bridge of Accumulating Responsibilities. This bridge covers an approximate age span from about twenty to forty years of age. While early adulthood, as I define it, covers this approximate age range, these are not hard and fast ages, rather it is a *stage* of adulthood.

The Three Phases of Early Adulthood

Early adulthood can be viewed as comprising one of 3 phases:

1. *The Beginning*
2. *Feet Firmly Planted*
3. *The Serious Climb*

Phase 1 - The Beginning

The first few years of adulthood are often like being a kid in a toy or candy store. There are the experiences of starting work or commencing a career, the thrill and relief of earning a pay check after years of being at school, meeting new colleagues and friends, new areas to learn through training at work and the education received through real world experiences. Also, there is the realization and need to relate and identify with a new business and social culture. This culture likely will include a set of standards, values and ethics that is imposed on adults different from being at college or that experienced as a teenager. These standards, values, and ethics will need to be followed or one will have to face the consequences at work, in society, within the family, or within your community.

This early stage of adulthood is a time to see how you fit in while experiencing the ebb and flow of work and life. It is also a period when one experiences the first tugs on our personal time as we may neglect old friends in favor of spending time with new colleagues that are integral to our work life. This phase is when we first learn whether we can survive and thrive in our career while juggling our relationships.

Phase 2 - Feet Firmly Planted

The next few years in this phase of early adulthood are less about exploration and more about stability. You may have your feet firmly planted and begun pursuing promotions at work as you undertake more meaningful roles at work, gather greater self-confidence in your social circles, and develop the skills to manage people, projects, and perhaps clients.

I have found that by around year five of your career or work experience, you are likely to have a good idea that you have chosen a profession, career, or work experience that you enjoy. If not, you are likely exploring alternatives in your career or at work that may be a better fit in terms of your culture, aspirations, and values.

You may also be approaching the point in your career where you start to gain a sense of whether what you are engaged in is worthy of the effort ahead. Pressure outside your career becomes more pronounced at this time as you may be in a serious relationship or married. Perhaps, you are also a new parent.

Phase 3 - The Serious Climb

The last phase of the early stage of adulthood I describe as the final climb. This is a final climb toward establishing yourself by starting to really know who you are and becoming comfortable within your own skin whether at home, at work, or in your career.

This phase often requires assuming more responsibility, handing larger, and more complex matters, and developing broader and deeper relationships. It is also a time when politics are at play either at work if you are rising fast or within your expanded family.

Even if you are not married by your mid to late thirties, you are likely to have seriously considered taking this step in your personal life. You also are likely to have begun to consider starting a family and commenced accumulating additional responsibilities such as purchasing a home or acquiring additional cars. This period culminates the three phases of early adulthood.

Why the Bridge of Accumulating Responsibilities?

I view all of these three phases in early adulthood as a period that is defined by accumulating responsibilities, which is why I have termed it the "Bridge of Accumulating Responsibilities". These responsibilities include those associated with owning assets, owing liabilities, having experiences and a wider range of emotions . These accumulations hopefully come with a payoff of financial reward and the psychological satisfaction of family growth and career advancement.

The journey across the Bridge of Accumulating Responsibilities is like all of life, never easy nor quick. In your twenties and thirties, we have a strong tendency to assume new responsibilities. These may be the responsibilities that come from a burgeoning career, committed relationships, getting married, raising children, acquiring a larger home and probably a larger mortgage, more cars, an increase for desired or needed vacations, increased credit card debt, etc.

Every generation that leaves their teens, passes through college, and enters into their twenties and thirties faces challenges. Baby boomers had to find their voices in the sixties and seventies, whether over civil rights, Vietnam, or their choice in clothes, music, or lifestyle. A few years ago, Gen X'ers and Millennials faced challenges arising from the Great Recession, especially the inability to find a job. The recession forced them to continue out of economic and financial necessity to live at home with their parents. Now while Gen X'ers and Millennials face their own unique challenges, Generation Z are beginning to experience theirs, and so it will go on for future generations who cross the bridge of accumulating responsibilities.

Challenges in Transitioning Across this Bridge

While young adults will hopefully transition easily across the "bridge of accumulating responsibilities," for some it may be perceived by them as a transition from a comfortable and stable home life to a lifestyle that is unchartered and lacking in structure. While the transition into adulthood and the independence that comes with it is exciting, it also comes with its own set of stressors. Individuals leaving a college and university setting may have expectations relating to starting their career of choice, launching a business, or perhaps settling down in marriage. These are life goals that we all look forward to, but that does not mean the transition doesn't come without its own set of challenges.

A career may include more extensive travel than at any time to date, intensive on-the-job training, a series of promotions with increasing responsibilities, greater accountability, more money than you have ever earned or handled, the need to team with colleagues who you would not choose as friends, having to report to supervisors, along with being managed and managing others.

These new responsibilities and challenges occur while continually managing new relationships with family and friends outside of work. I coined this bridge "accumulating responsibilities" in part because of my own experience, but as much because of what I have observed through people who have worked for me, with me, or in conjunction with mentoring my children and their friends.

It is a natural evolution to acquire "things" in your twenties, thirties, or later as your life and career are built. However, accumulation brings stress and can cause imbalance between a career and your personal life. Often, careers are placed as a priority while relationships suffer.

The challenges that young adults can be faced with when navigating the "Bridge of Accumulating Responsibilities" might include:

- *Being authentic and personal while maintaining professionalism*
- *Understanding and handling burnout*
- *The consequences of perfectionism*
- *Handling toxic practices and relationships*
- *Managing difficult colleagues and clients*
- *Career and compensation aspirations and expectations meshed with reality*
- *Work-Life balance challenges*

Each of these challenges presents stress stemming from the fact that at this stage of life our expectations may be out of balance with our reality. We expect to develop our futures, complete with more meaningful relationships and lasting careers. Yet, what happens if these life goals aren't achieved overnight? How long do we patiently wait before happiness is thwarted? These aspirations are important to be able to navigate across this bridge. However, the same issues may come back to haunt you in midlife if they are not properly addressed in a lifestyle that does not seem to be satisfactorily fulfilled.

The Wearing of the "Mask" Concealing True Self-Identity

The journey during which we navigate our twenties and thirties is a time when we transition from a relatively carefree college existence to one that is often career and relationship focused. This is when success can be defined not by what surrounds our lives, but rather, how we fit into our surroundings and what material possessions we have accumulated.

During this period of young adulthood, we also perfect the wearing of a mask that we acquired in adolescence in order to be accepted by friends. Now in our twenties and thirties, we define ourselves by what we do, who we have as our friends, what clubs we attend, restaurants we frequent, etc. Yet, we do not always define ourselves by who we are. The mask is important as quite often, we wear it throughout traversing this bridge during this stage of adulthood only to really address removing it to be more authentic when we experience our midlife.

As I have pointed out, there comes a time when the "mask" we have worn since adolescence, the one that we put on to be liked and project who we want to be perceived as, must eventually come off to find our true self, which in turn, can lead to sustained happiness. This revealing of the mask is the story of the Midlife Bridge. One reason we often do not address our true self and authenticity until midlife is that during adulthood, when we are on the Bridge of Accumulating Responsibilities, we are often too externally focused with little breathing room or self-introspection time to take the mask off.

Aren't my twenties and thirties time for fun, pleasure, and purpose?

No matter our age or stage of life, throughout adulthood there should be a constant desire to pursue your passions with a balance unique for you to seek pleasure and purpose in your life.

How many people have we observed during one's twenties or thirties, where it seems that often there is an excess of pleasure without sufficient meaning in one's life?

Enjoyment or pleasure should be viewed as hedonistic experiences and are short lived, e.g. enjoying a nice meal. Purpose, on the other hand, is a eudemonic experience and long lasting as it provides a sense of meaning.

The constant interaction unique to each person between the hedonistic and eudemonic experiences can produce sustained happiness. This theory was written about in *"Happiness by Design:Finding Pleasure and Purpose in Everyday Life"* by Paul Dolan, which theorized the science behind positive psychology and the benefits gained from enhancing your wellbeing.

In all probability when traveling across the Bridge of Accumulating Responsibilities, one may find that pleasurable experiences can provide momentary feelings of happiness, but these do not last long because the pleasure is dependent upon external events and experiences. Often, we have to keep on having these "good" experiences in order to feel pleasure such as more money, sex, alcohol, drugs, food, etc. Thus, one can become addicted to these external experiences, needing more and more to fuel a short-lived feeling of happiness, which soon returns to the level of happiness prior to the hedonistic experience of pleasure. What is important is that each person should, and no doubt does experience hedonistic pleasures that are not addictive behaviors such as an evening at the theater or perhaps even the quintessential bar of chocolate.

What has been well researched is that experiencing pleasures, no matter how enjoyable and even if not addictive, without having a sense of purpose in your life is not sufficient to achieve a state of sustained happiness.

In my view, sustained happiness is a state of mind. It is a reflection of what goes on inside of ourselves as we experience both pleasures and purpose that create the right personal mix that achieves a state of sustained happiness. Thus, no amount of partying, socializing, or external experiences will produce sustained happiness until a person stops looking outside of themselves.

As I previously wrote, possessing a sense of purpose or meaning is one of the core elements of positive psychology (PERMAH). Possessing a sense of purpose is fundamental to a meaningful human life, but as I noted, it also requires the experiences of pleasure to enhance wellbeing to bring sustained happiness within oneself.

Think of it this way. A life of purpose with little pleasure may be viewed as dull while one that is mostly hedonistic and full of pleasure, but without purpose can feel empty. It is important to find the right combination of hedonistic and eudemonic experiences (pleasures and purpose) for each person in their personal combination that works for them.

Aristotle, around two thousand years ago, wrote of happiness and pleasure, stating, "*Happiness is not to be found in pleasant amusements, rather happiness is activity in accordance with the highest virtue.*" As to what was the highest virtue, Aristotle focused on that which is noble and divine. Today, we may interpret this as having a sense of meaning or purpose.

Thus, surely it is better to begin early as an adult to focus on understanding your passions, what provides you a sense of purpose, and finding the right balance with pleasure rather than figure it out when faced with the stresses and challenges that will be presented to you in midlife or later? When the right balance is not sought between pleasure and purpose and hedonistic experiences are too plentiful, it can be painful to fall off the "bridge". While this can occur at all stages of life, drug and alcohol addictions and other examples of pleasure fixes are far too common while crossing this first bridge in adulthood. If one succumbs to these, it will require painful remediation to be able to traverse the "Bridge of Accumulating Responsibilities" successfully.

Understanding When You May have Crossed this Bridge

As you traverse the "Bridge of Accumulating Responsibilities," no doubt a time will arise when you may seek to understand whether you are getting close to the end of this bridge.

As young adults, we are often observed as bursting with energy and enthusiasm. After living perhaps carefree years as a teenager, we take on adult life and immerse ourselves in it. Yet, we often make decisions in young adulthood that can haunt us in midlife or later. These decisions include spending time with children, giving time and attention to a spouse, and taking care of one's own body and mind.

When we start to internally raise these questions and begin to ponder their answers, we may be at the cusp of entering midlife. These questions are part of challenges we face in midlife that are addressed in the next chapter. Thus, we transition from the Bridge of Accumulating Responsibilities to the Midlife Bridge by addressing things we wish we could change or living a life we wish we could change.

Today, Gen X'ers, Millennials, and now Generation Z possess the education, technical know-how, diversity, and ease to access information that enables them to rethink and revolutionize their experiences as they age. These generations display their desire to focus on longer lives, health and wellness, the environment, a redefined balance between work, play and education with a different financial security focus than Baby Boomers. But to find sustained happiness, they will also need to focus on lifelong learning, lifelong work, lifelong giving, lifelong loving, lifelong investing, and lifelong health maintenance.

What is notable about Millennials is that they seek a sense of purpose in what they do from an early age. It has been written quite extensively that Millennials are more inclined than earlier generations to define their purpose and act on it early in their lives, including volunteerism, mentoring, and other meaningful activities. Millennials faced tough economic waters as they matured into adults. By taking on their generation's challenges, Millennials or Gen Z are perhaps better positioned than Baby Boomers or even Gen X to traverse the Bridge of Accumulating Responsibilities and permit them to progress through adulthood with self-empowerment and a sense of purpose. This is what equips them well to navigate the Bridge of Accumulating Responsibilities.

Concluding Reflections

As a Baby Boomer, I have personally learned from generations that have come after me, how Gen X, Millennials and Gen Z, passionately adopt social causes, quickly adopt a sense of meaning, or redefine work/life balance. Maybe because they did not have to fight for their voice like baby boomers did in the 1960s, they are using their voice in a way that is just as impressive or indeed more so, than baby boomers who found a need to resort to violence, strife, and upheaval that we witnessed in the 1960s and 1970s.

Some researchers have suggested that Baby Boomers with many now crossing the later bridges of "Midlife" or "Decumulation and Simplicity," may have been just as passionate about something in their youth and had an affinity to a cause that gave them meaning, but gave it up as they aged. I have found in my work with my clients that passions from earlier in your life (often from your teens and early to mid-twenties), are still a burning passion in midlife, but simply need rekindling.

So, a word of advice...Never forget and suppress what you are passionate about early in your adulthood as it may come back to be a very valuable fire to reignite within you as you get older. Pursuing your passions can position you well for navigating my three metaphorical bridges.

Now that we have addressed traversing the Bridge of Accumulating Responsibilities, it is an appropriate time to address the Midlife Bridge.

SIX

THE MIDLIFE BRIDGE

I t's likely that we all know someone who we perceive has failed to address their midlife and perhaps is in the midst of a "midlife crisis." To avoid this particular crisis happening to ourselves, we need to understand what and when is midlife and then, how to handle the challenges and issues associated with it.

My view is that midlife is not age based, but stage based. Midlife is the bridge we navigate after we have traversed the "bridge of accumulating responsibilities," and as we glide into midlife.

Midlife as a concept is not new. In fact, it has been around for a long time.

The History of Midlife

Over a wide swathe of centuries, many distinguished authors and philosophers have described the various stages of man. The compartmentalization of human life into a series of "ages" has been commonplace in both art and literature across many civilizations. For example, the "seven ages of man" was a term used many centuries ago and was derived from medieval philosophy. In fact, King Henry V ordered a tapestry to be made illustrating the seven ages of man.

In the fourteenth century, the Italian poet Dante confronted midlife as the "dark unknown in the search for a right path towards a meaningful life." The opening line in Dante's great work, "The Divine Comedy," is:

"Midway life's journey I was made aware; That I had strayed into a dark forest; And the right path appeared not anywhere."

Dante referred to being in midlife and feeling trapped by not seeing a clear path out. About 700 years after Dante, despite changes in the way we live, we continue to travel through the unsettling experience of midlife. But hopefully, we offset it with self-introspection while traveling through the inner paths within ourselves.

For purposes to place some definition around middle age, midlife may be viewed as occurring somewhere between the ages of 40 and 60-years-old. However, as stated earlier, I believe it is more stage than age based. In the United States, this age band can represent about a third of the population, but this age band can represent as much as 70 percent of the country's wealth.

Throughout most of human history, middle age has been experienced as a time of decline and decay. Certainly, until around the middle of the twentieth century, human psychological growth and development was thought to be complete by young adulthood, and life after approximately 40 or 50-years of age was regarded as a time of decline and retirement. Obviously, much has changed as we now experience significantly increased life longevity.

One hundred and fifty years ago, the concept or indeed the use of the words midlife or middle age would have baffled Westerners as the concept had not been invented! Prior to 1900, the U.S. Census Bureau did not even ask for one's year of birth. Life expectancy was short at just over 40 years.

Middle age is an idea that was invented as a concept in the second half of the nineteenth century. Today, midlife is at the center of American society. In many respects, the concept of middle age in America mirrors America's entry onto the world stage. The industrial revolution, new laws protecting workers, some advances in medicine, and a more prosperous life along with perhaps a slightly longer life expectancy, gave rise to a more affluent and vocal middle class. P.

Cohen, author of *"In Our Prime: The Reinvention of Middle Age,"* summarized middle age as "a kind of never-never-land, a place that you never want to enter or never want to leave."

Two themes run throughout the history of middle age. The first is the constant struggle over how it is defined and by whom. The second theme concerns the tension between the notion of self-help's ability to empower or manipulate. On the second theme, western society has predominately chosen the route of personal improvement; however, midlife is often met with resignation or regret. It seems few are eager to receive their AARP membership card. It is no wonder there are so many self-help books and blogs that now exist on the subject of midlife.

Midlife Crisis: Fact or Fallacy?

The phrase "midlife crisis" was aptly coined by Canadian psychologist Elliot Jacques in his 1965 article, "Death and the Midlife Crisis," written and published for the International Journal of Psychoanalysis. However, he first described this concept back in 1957 in London for the British Psycho-Analytical Society. He was not the first to discuss a "midlife crisis." As I mention elsewhere, Dante Alighieri's 14th Century Divine Comedy addressed midlife centuries ago. Yet, whether midlife crises actually happen is debatable.

What is more likely is that adults experience a midlife slump and late-life upswing, and actual levels of happiness vary from person to person and county to country. Jonathan Rauch in his book, "The Happiness Curve," covered this topic. During the period closely resembling the Bridge of Accumulating Responsibilities, in our late 30s and 40s, it is a stressful period of juggling careers, children, parents, and expenses. These swamp the dreams of youth and can make one miserable and create a midlife slump. This, in turn, helps us to rethink our priorities and aspirations since as we age, we are more capable of accepting what we cannot control. Thus, we become wiser, calmer, and more pragmatic after working through the slump or as I term it, the midlife bridge. After all, research between age and wellbeing by University of Southern

California psychologist, Arthur Stone, shows that after hitting 50 most people feel less regretful about their past and more positive about their lives in general. Indeed, when asked in their 50s and 60s if they would like to be 20 again, most strongly preferred to be the age they are today.

When does midlife occur?

The question I am asked perhaps more than any other is, "When does midlife occur?"

Before I undertook my doctoral research, I suppose I too was unsure. Looking back, it probably seems to many that we glide into midlife. Perhaps for some, psychologically it is your 40th birthday. For others, seeing those grey hairs multiply, or for some, realizing that going to bed at 9:30 p.m. is more satisfying than staying up past midnight signals it.

The reality is that the age upon when we may enter midlife may likely change as we live longer. Yet, all of us will surely experience midlife as we age.

Life Events that Can Trigger a Midlife Introspection

Most people experience life events such as the death of close friends and family members, divorces, health scares, and job losses that can trigger a self-introspection of one's life. The posing of a question such as "what's next," and often the commencement of a journey to reinvent or rewire oneself, occurs next to achieve a lifestyle of choice.

The reason that these triggers may initiate a self-introspection during one's midlife is because of the confluence of three midlife challenges that can impact us. It is the recognition of these challenges that more likely signify the importance of midlife rather than the absolute age (e.g. 40) or the accumulation of grey hairs.

Three Distinct Midlife Challenges

During midlife, it is likely that we may experience three distinct challenges. How intense they are to each person will of course vary, as well as how we handle them. The three challenges are:

- *Physiological*
- *Interpersonal*
- *Intrapersonal*

The physiological challenge is the realization that one's body, stamina, libido, and cardio functions are not what they were in our unbridled years of the early stage of adulthood. This physiological challenge hits us in midlife when our weight may slowly increase and accumulate in areas we don't like, lines may form that never existed on our face or body beforehand, grey hairs sprout and in vanity moments, we cover them up. We are still very active and healthy, but our sprinting cannot match that of our twenties and perhaps, we tire more easily.

Even top athletes like tennis pro Roger Federer will be pressed to compete with the very best in his forties. Mind you, at this age we are still good, but not at our physiological peak. For most of us, we accept this change and adjust or adapt. However, for some, it's a pressure to look youthful given all of the tools and techniques offered. Don't get me wrong, eating healthily and exercising are key to our vitality; however, no cosmetic surgery, vitamin regimen, or exercise program will keep us young. They just make us feel younger until the day we recognize and then accept that we are older than we were in our twenties and thirties and physiologically we have changed.

The outward signs of aging are a constant reminder, even if not consciously, of our mortality. Changes in cardiovascular efficiency, slower responses, and the gradual decline in our athletic ability or lowered libido are all factors that impact men and women who are in midlife.

The second challenge are the interpersonal challenges. As we move into our forties and fifties, we start to recognize and realize that our parents are aging, need more help or unfortunately, pass away. Our children are no longer children, but are becoming young adults who then move away to college, which in itself can be a traumatic life event for a parent. Indeed, our spouse may no longer look and act like the spouse we remember twenty years earlier. These are all part of life and happen to all of us. For some, we take these changes in our stride, yet for others stress may ensue from any of the above life events.

Long-term personal commitments such as one's marriage may become stale and contentious due to routine and predictability. Divorces can often occur in midlife, which most likely will create stress, just as relationships can be stressed when children go off to college or parents age and fall ill. Indeed, as one's parents age, role reversal can occur and the child in midlife can become the parent.

When any or all of the above occur during midlife, we become aware of our own life timeline and deeper within our mortality due to what we observe and experience from these life events in midlife along our journey through adulthood.

We may also experience a third challenge — those that are intrapersonal in nature. When we crossed the "bridge of accumulating responsibilities," we matured our dreams and aspirations for a career, spouse, family, children, financial success, and a host of other passions and pursuits. As most of us find out, life intervenes in our ability to achieve all we aspire to. Again, for many, we adapt and move on. For some, coming up short can be stressful, disappointing, and can cause grief over a loss of a dream. As examples, being passed over for a promotion, not having the career we imagined, the home we really want, or indeed the family we wished for can cause one to sense a loss of an aspiration and look inward during midlife to be introspective about one's life.

Midlife and the Relationship with Time

One of the most profound changes during midlife is our relationship with time. While we may find that we finally achieve our goals from young adulthood, we may also feel that the reality didn't live up to the dream. This gives rise to disillusionment. Often, we come to realize that the dream was not ours in the first place, but one instilled in us by a parent, mentor, or spouse.

A Midlife Introspection

When all three challenges present themselves, all it takes in my view, is a trigger to cause an introspection. This trigger is most likely a life event such as the death of a parent, the loss of form as a top athlete, a job loss, or children leaving home. This is the trigger that may cause the midlife introspection. Alternatively, we may quickly move past with the life event and move on with our life or it may cause one to rebel against reality and be in denial that one is on the "midlife bridge". This is the so called "midlife crisis."

Issues Faced in Midlife

Anyone can experience stress from the three challenges described earlier. It can happen to anyone, regardless of gender, race, or social status. It is life!

Because experiencing midlife has unique characteristics to each person, the issues that may arise from the three challenges during midlife will always need to be addressed in a way unique to each person. Some of the issues that are likely in need to be addressed can include:

- *Aspects of aging and longevity*
- *The fear of losing the past*
- *The fear of having mis-lived the past*
- *The fear of accepting the present*
- *The need to address one's self-identity by revealing one's true self at work and at home*
- *Facing one's mortality*
- *Addressing one's legacy*
- *How to genuinely pursue one's passions and gain a true sense of purpose*

These are not lightweight issues to tackle!

Midlife and Identity Issues

Midlife is such a powerful time of our adulthood that several identity crises can occur in midlife if the issues outlined from any or all of the three challenges are not addressed.

During midlife we can experience identity crises in a variety of ways:

- *An overly centralized focus on one's occupational identity;*
- *Experiences of identity threat by being defined by what we do, not who we are;*
- *Damage to one's self-esteem by the questioning of one's self-worth;*
- *Trying to finding meaning through providing services;*
- *Belonging to a professional community to gain self-identity;*
- *A loss of identity by the sale of one's business or practice or by passing the baton onto successors*
- *One's self-efficacy and the questioning of one's competence;*
- *Experiences of aging in a society indifferent to aging;*
- *Coping with late-career transitions, but having difficulty reimagining the self.*

When we personally seek answers to midlife questions, midlife challenges, or midlife issues, we may find out that our own course, to date, was not well charted. Perhaps, we never set the right goals or more accurately, we may have set and pursued the goals that best defined our purpose in life at the time we set them earlier in adulthood, but now those have changed.

I personally faced all three challenges. I experienced a combination of physiological changes after I turned 50. I ran less frequently to save my knees, was a little slower, and gradually changed my cardio work to spinning. I was also impacted by changes in some of my most important interpersonal relationships, especially because of the death of my daughter when I was 55. Finally, I experienced an intrapersonal challenge when my career collapsed with Arthur Andersen's demise when I was 49.

These events triggered my own introspection to address how to bounce back from the losses and how to look to enjoy the second half of my adult life.

Working through identity issues such as defining yourself by who you are rather than by what you do, may help. Such an introspection may result in the conclusion to focus on being more aligned with or the revealing of one's true self. In other words, the quest to be more authentic and focus on how you can live your life to be defined by who you are, not by what you do.

Revealing the True Self...Seeking Authenticity in the Second Half of Life

A major life event can be the trigger to knock the wind out of our sails. We may ask ourselves, as I did, "What's next?" or "Is this all there is?" This introspection is the beginning of a journey on the Midlife Bridge to reveal the true self.

When significant life events occur, they can become triggers that result in a self-introspection. We find ourselves looking inward and judging whether we are happy with who we are. For many, it may be a moment for a private realization in which we feel we have come up short and have compromised ourselves in choice of career, spouse, or our own values and desires. This can be a thought or conclusion that can be self-detrimental because midlife is an important time and stage of life.

The journey across the "Midlife Bridge" neither starts with a jolt, nor ends abruptly. It weaves into your life and sails out, sometimes without one being aware of the beginning or end of midlife happening. The "Midlife Bridge" is key to our journey into the second half of life and the revealing of one's true self.

Three eminent psychologists, among many, have addressed the second half of life and they are: Carl Jung, Erik Erikson, and Daniel Levinson.

These three psychologists and others, all framed midlife as a period of difficult choices and challenges. In effect, it is the crossover point of one's life journey. There is no consensus on when midlife passage occurs, which validates why I believe, it is stage based.

During midlife many people find themselves caring for both children and aging parents while juggling their careers with these responsibilities. As a result, it is not uncommon to experience a lot of stress and an "expectations gap" that can develop in midlife when we may feel that we didn't measure up to the goals of our youth. However, as we age, we become more realistic about goals and more satisfied with what we achieve. By the time we reach our 60s, we are more inclined to live in the present and focus on our personal relationships and less on success as measured by society and peers. One's satisfaction with life is driven by unmet aspirations that are painfully felt during midlife, but are gladly discarded and felt with less regret in our 60s, 70s, and beyond.

Therefore, by selecting to focus on gaining greater purpose in our life and placing relationships at the forefront of our lives as careers recede, these steps become integral to a life reinvention.

Anyone can work to become the person they have always wanted to be, or in other words, be authentic to one's true self. That is not to say it's easy work; however, it would be interesting to contemplate a society that allows people to be valued because of who they are, not judged by how old they are.

Carl Jung believed that it is the unfolding of the self that can facilitate a midlife reinvention, as he believed that midlife distress (such as the three challenges highlighted earlier) are an unpleasant but healthy and essential step for psychological growth. Jung further believed that the gift of life's second half is the awakening and symbolic transformation associated with the death of our youthful self and the awakening of the soul.

It is this powerful recognition that occurs during a self-introspection in one's midlife that causes someone to recognize the challenges and commence dealing with them. By letting go of one's youth and looking within, thus begins the journey to reveal the true self. This true self involves seeking authenticity and is a much different journey than the first half of life, which involves childhood, adolescence, and the journey across the Bridge of Accumulating Responsibilities.

Midlife – Facing Mortality and Embracing Spirituality

Midlife is a time during our adulthood when a significant life event can be a trigger that can cause an introspection, but it can also create a confrontation of one's own mortality - an essential step in revealing one's true self. This confrontation is a step in the recognition of one's own life timeline as we understand and sense the horizon of our own journey and we realize that we are mortal. In turn, we begin to really understand the importance that legacy possesses in one's life, which shapes the prioritizing of our values and the need to reorient oneself to focus on gaining a greater sense of purpose or meaning.

A self-introspection often causes someone to become more spiritual or seek more spirituality in one's life. Spirituality can act as an embracing force that can include gaining a greater sense of purpose, being more altruistic, and addressing one's own mortality. An emphasis on spirituality is characterized by an increased focus on how we experience ourselves in the world.

"Vertical spirituality" describes our desire to transcend the individual ego while "horizontal spirituality" is the desire to be of service to other humans and the planet. A pursuit of spirituality is an on-going journey most likely characterized by an intense, consuming motivation to "become," by which we elicit transformative experiences of ourselves and the world. It becomes how we create a sense of purpose or meaning in that person's life as well as those around that person.

From a wider perspective about adulthood, the first half of a person's life is focused on establishing personal identity, creating boundaries, and seeking security. These are often externally focused in building a family or a career. This contrasts with the journey of the second half of life which involves a search for the true self and unlike the first half, is often far more internally focused.

Midlife - Removing the "Mask"

While navigating the Midlife Bridge, a critical part of the journey is the removing of one's "mask" to permit one to be more authentic.

As teenagers, many of us put on a "mask" in order to be liked by the "cool kids" at school. Yet, we continue to wear the mask after high school, through university, and into our careers. We may not publicly admit that we wear a mask, but how many of us aren't happy because our true self is hidden. We also define ourselves as young adults by what we do, who we know, what clubs we belong to, and introduce ourselves by our profession as a means of being accepted or revered. However, defining oneself by what you do (lawyer, doctor, or accountant, as an example), is not defining yourself by who you are. It is this journey to take off the mask and expose your real self, that is neither easy nor quick, but the hallmark of the journey across the "Midlife Bridge."

Concluding Reflections

Unlike the Bridge of Accumulating Responsibilities or the Bridge of Decumulation and Simplicity that follows the Midlife Bridge, the time spent traversing the Midlife Bridge is a time for one to step back and evaluate one's life, one's identity, the dreams from one's youth, a focus on the goals that are still realistic, and a desire to abandon illusions. It is a unique opportunity of enhancing self-awareness and developing or refining a sense of purpose.

As we have seen, a trigger from a significant life event can provoke an intense introspection that can create a desire to reinvent oneself. Midlife can be an intense personal struggle to come to terms with the physiological, psychological, career and relational changes that are occurring, yet midlife is an opportunity or catalyst for accomplishing amazing personal growth and potential transformation during the second half of life.

This is why we likely might notice so many people in their forties, fifties, and sixties attending retreats, switching careers, and doing what they hope will provide them with a sense of purpose as well as pleasure.

Taking off the mask is often a challenge, particularly if we hang onto our career as a constant while we undergo personal challenges. It is only after we have addressed taking off the mask that we can determine if we are truly happy in our career or need to make a change.

However, often by the time we get to that point, we may be faced with only a short time before retirement. If not, it may become the right time when we feel comfortable to rewire our life and pursue an encore career.

The Midlife Bridge is not easy to navigate. It takes courage to address mortality, unveil your true self, strive for authenticity and seek what will make you happy. However, once the "Midlife Bridge" has been crossed, you will find yourself on the next bridge, "The Bridge of Decumulation and Simplicity."

SEVEN

THE BRIDGE OF DECUMULATION AND SIMPLICITY

M aybe during the middle of the twentieth century you retired, received a pen, a pension, and a party. No more. Now it is a time for transition to new challenges, pathways, and accomplishments and this is what the "Bridge of Decumulation and Simplicity" is about.

The midlife introspection has occurred, and you are intent on revealing your true self, which plays a significant role in traversing this metaphorical bridge.

Unlike the Bridge of Accumulating Responsibilities, which is externally focused, the Bridge of Decumulation and Simplicity is internally focused. The removal of the mask and the unveiling of one's true self involves realizing that happiness comes from within. Deep and meaningful relationships are important along with pursuing passions that are purposeful. The materialistic assets accumulated in earlier life become less relevant or of value. It is this realization that arises from a self-introspection during midlife and it is the journey to be authentic that hallmarks this third metaphorical bridge.

During this time, children have grown up and left the home, so downsizing the home and shedding many years of accumulated assets is often a signature point of this bridge. The need to gain happiness by having acquired expensive toys also has lost relevance. There is a diminished need and desire for second homes, expensive cars, and expensive jewelry. Of course, if one has financial security, then retaining these assets to enjoy with close family and friends plays an important role in later life. However, if financial security is a concern, given an increased longevity, then such assets are shed. Also, relationships that are toxic are ended. A lifestyle of choice often is crafted to achieve sustained happiness, achieved by enhanced wellbeing while traversing this metaphorical bridge.

We start our journey across the Bridge of Decumulation and Simplicity between the approximate ages of 60 and 80 years, and of course, after crossing the Midlife Bridge. As in the other bridges, it is more stage based than age based.

Having faced and addressed the challenges that may arise during midlife at this later stage of adulthood, we become more focused on the issues of aging and longevity, which become preeminent factors in influencing one's life and lifestyle.

You often hear that people in their sixties and seventies, after many years of a demanding career, child rearing, or supporting aging parents, state they want a simpler life. This does not mean retiring. It does mean rewiring the way we think and behave and reinventing what we do. It involves shedding those people, responsibilities, and assets that add little to your wellbeing or indeed even detract and cause it to suffer. Putting our quest to reinvent or rewire into action after a midlife introspection is what the Bridge of Decumulation and Simplicity is all about.

Aging and Longevity

Today, we face a longer lifespan than any generation before us. Aging has become not just a fact of life, but an industry, and longevity not just a time span, but an economy. Of course, getting old has been a reality since the beginning of humankind. However, one thing that has changed is the perception and definition of when one is considered old.

Dante Alighieri, c. 1265 – 1321, was an Italian poet of the Late Middle Ages. His *Divine Comedy* is widely considered the most important poem of the Middle Ages and the greatest Italian literary work. Dante perceived that in his time, being an old man began at 45.

According to a recent survey by YouGov, Britons have very clearly defined definitions of youth, middle, and old age. For young people, youth is not so fleeting after all as it lasts throughout one's twenties, and being "young" begins to wane at 29, according to the survey. Once you reach 30, you are no longer considered young by the majority of Brits and have officially entered the next phase of life. Reminiscent of crossing various bridges?

The ages between 30 and 47 don't quite fit into any category according to the survey, although 30-year-olds are no longer "young" adults at this point. The good news is they are not exactly middle-aged either. Rather, they have entered "a no-man's land age group – an age range that the English language doesn't seem to have a term for." According to the survey, most Britons don't believe a person has become middle-aged until they reach at least 48 and old age doesn't set in until 70.

My conclusion is that age really is just a number and is more stage based. Interestingly, the United Nations and most scientists define old age as commencing at 60. By 2029, all Baby Boomers will be 65 years or over, assuming Baby Boomer years ended in 1964. Millennials are now the largest generation group and the percentage of corporate leadership positions held by Baby Boomers is continuing to drop as this generation ages.

Here are some additional relevant statistics:

- In 2015 there were more than 800 million people over the age of 60 on the planet and this will increase to about 2 billion by mid-century.
- Over the 35-year period from 2015 to 2050, the number of people aged 80 years old or older will quadruple to around 400 million people.
- There are now more global centenarians than the entire population of Iceland (which is about 319,000).
- Adults aged 65 years or older will outnumber children under the age of 16 by 2050. Perhaps we should recognize

that the world is bracing itself for the economic and social consequences of greater longevity.

- Paul Irving referenced in his book, *The Upside of Aging: How Long is Life Changing the World of Health, Work, Innovation, Policy and Purpose* that the number of people aged 60 years or older is projected to increase from 605 million to 2 billion between 2000 and 2050. Over the same period, the number of people aged 80 years or older will have quadrupled to 395 million, and adults aged 65 and over will outnumber children under the age of 14. Finally, another interesting statistic in the book is that in 1910, a Chilean female had a life expectancy of 33 years; it is now 82.
- In the United States, 10,000 people a day are turning 65.
- By approximately 2040, the 60 plus population will increase from 765 million to about 1.7 billion, according to the Milken Institute in 2015.

All of these statistics drive the need to assess the demographic implications as the numbers speak to both increased longevity and the swelling ranks of people in midlife and older.

Most impressive has been the climb in life expectancy. Throughout most of the history of the human race, worldwide life expectation was only 18. In 1900 it was 47 years of age, whereas today it is around 79 and continues to rise. Life expectancy is such that we now live at least 20 to 30 years beyond what was traditionally thought of as retirement age. We are in a new longevity economy.

While there are many facets to aging, former President Obama stated that aging was an opportunity for all Americans to have a shot at achieving their dreams at any age. In the United States and across the globe, there is fortunately a growing awareness about the abilities and capabilities of older adults, and thus the upside to aging.

The key question to me is: Are we prepared to live to the age of 100?

We should all be ready for the economic and social consequences of greater longevity. It is because of the increased longevity that the

Bridge of Decumulation and Simplicity may be as long, if not a longer runway than the other two bridges.

A Brief History of Retirement

Because of a much shorter life expectancy than exists today, there was no real concept of retirement until the latter half of the nineteenth century. As the size, breadth, and influence of the middle class rose with the industrialized revolution throughout the western world, masses of people found themselves with more money, time, and greater aspirations. As the middle class rose, so did life expectancy. Health care improved and consequently, people lived longer. Around 1870 and upon the reunification of Germany, Count Otto von Bismarck, Chancellor of Germany, worked to appease those impacted by the reunification and to mollify workers by initiating the world's first retirement plan with a small state pension at age 60. This was against the backdrop of a life expectancy of almost twenty years less (just over 40 years of age).

Great Britain adopted a similar retirement concept a few years later than Germany and established a small state pension at age 65. One hundred and fifty years later, we still use 65, or close to it, as a bench-mark for retirement. However, life expectancy has risen from just over 40 to just under 80.

Clearly, using the retirement models from the 19th century, one's retirement age should be in one's late nineties, but it isn't of course.

This fact established for me, the rationale behind the Bridge of Decumulation and Simplicity. The reality is that today, after working for many decades, as one approaches sixty year of age and faced with living perhaps another 30 years, considerable thought should be given to how we live into one's sixties, seventies, eighties, and beyond. It is this thought process and the time available, that leads to following a path of seeking authenticity and placing value on what is important to you in your life and shedding that which is not — thus, the rationale for the Bridge of Decumulation and Simplicity. When you arrive at this bridge, shedding people, assets, and the many moving parts to your life to achieve simplicity and a focus on what is important becomes paramount for many — hence, the name of my third metaphorical bridge.

I want to place this third metaphorical bridge into context with one's passage across the Midlife Bridge. During the Midlife Bridge, one has faced, addressed, and hopefully understood one's mortality and also understood why the desire to reveal the true self and address any physiological, interpersonal, and intrapersonal challenges.

A Fresh View of Retirement

Retirement also needs a fresh approach as we age and live longer. The policy of mandatory retirement influenced me while at Arthur Andersen, as it was enforced at 56 years old, surely today, this is far too young to be asked to formally retire? However, similar policies are still in place at many large CPA firms, although the mandatory retirement age that is often enforced is around the ages of 60 to 62. Mandatory retirement is also true at some leading law firms in the United States as well across a wide range of businesses. If your life expectancy is chasing 90, that could mean 25 plus years after mandatory retirement, a lot of time to reshape, rethink, and rewire your lifestyle.

There are obviously sound business reasons for having a retirement age, but that does not mean one retires to a sedate, quiet and non-productive life, unless you want that. There is a whole world to explore and be productive in, and if you properly rewire at the right time of your life during this stage of adulthood, the world can be your oyster.

Fortunately, traditional retirement is being reimagined. People can now reinvent themselves for a lifestyle that can last decades, when for example they may be retiring from professional practice.

I feel strongly that age should not be a barrier to being able to work whether in your sixties, seventies, eighties or beyond, as long as you can be an effective contributor. In fact, some countries are embracing the economic opportunities that can be derived from an older workforce.

Concluding Reflections

The Bridge of Decumulation and Simplicity, given our longevity, can be viewed as the journey of the second half of your life, living by being one's true self and by being authentic. In my opinion, the journey across the third metaphorical bridge is influenced by the reality of a longer life span than previous generations, the need or desire to work, even if part time, and the necessity to secure a financial future based upon living much longer than we have historically.

So, it is not surprising that an increasing number of people do not retire. They may "retire" from jobs that have mandatory retirement ages or from careers they have been immersed in for decades. However, faced with many viable years ahead of us, many people take on encore careers, second acts, or part time vocations. Hopefully, such roles and positions provide a sense of purpose, which as we have seen, is important for enhancing one's wellbeing.

We likely know people who have turned to encore careers or not-for-profit positions. In effect, they are rewiring their lives and rein-venting their careers.

Personally, I believe that the term "retirement" should be replaced with "rewirement" as the mantra for what one may do in one's sixties or beyond. Rewiring how we think and behave for the next 30 years with a focus on living a lifestyle of choice by being authentic and enjoying meaningful encore careers, and advanced re-education are all constituents of the actions that occur while traversing the Bridge of Decumulation and Simplicity. Of course, along with pursuing the above is the shedding of parts of your life that are inconsistent with your lifestyle of choice, that thus signify the decumulation and simplicity desired in your life.

EIGHT

PROFESSIONAL WELLBEING

A s previously described, when the science of positive psychology is applied, it allows us to thrive by enhancing our wellbeing.

Having practiced as a professional service provider for decades, I thought that writing a chapter about professional wellbeing would be worthy of how and why understanding positive psychology can enhance your career.

Through applying the science to your life and your practice, you can enhance your wellbeing, which will not only help you personally thrive, but be of value to those in any practice you belong to and enable your career to thrive as well. This is what I call *"Professional Wellbeing."*

Wellbeing and Your Career

As a professional service provider, the notion of addressing my well-being while I was building my career was way off my radar screen. I was focused on learning and building my technical skills, how to develop clients and bring in business, keep clients happy, and under-stand the politics of practice and be perceived as successful in my career. Being happy was never addressed.

My training and education was extensive as Arthur Andersen probably had one of the strongest training and development programs of any firm, anywhere in the world with fabulous values and a culture that was highly respected. To this day, Andersen is or was, one of the greatest place to work at and I was proud to be a partner.

However, from the 1970s through the 1990s, the idea of focusing on one's wellbeing was not an area of focus in career development. As the science of positive psychology has developed over the past twenty years, many more firms have come to understand the substantial benefits achieved from applying the science. So, it is no wonder that professional service firms, especially global accounting firms, such as PWC, are establishing wellbeing programs.

The notion of enhancing one's wellbeing, might sound a little "woo-woo" to a professional service provider or firm, until you unwrap positive psychology and understand the benefits that can be achieved.

Why a Coach May Help You Thrive in Your Career

Here is my perspective on why a professional should consider a coach to embrace positive psychology to develop his or her career and personal wellbeing.

Have you ever seen a world class tennis player or football team without a coach? Coaches focus on performance and not just the physical performance, but the mental and spiritual aspects too. Coaches and players undertake this relationship between them so that the mind, body, and spirit are aligned. Service professionals, like professional athletes, thus may need to hire a coach to take their performance to the next level.

I personally believe that positive psychology coaching can assist a professional to train the brain to make the changes in behaviors and mindset that can result in improved wellbeing.

As a professional service provider, one might not practice their skill set in the same way that professional sports figures practice technical mastery. Professionals may not practice running sprints, but they should practice mastery of relationship building.

People with careers can benefit, at the right time, by utilizing coaches just as actors, tennis players, and singers do. I am not referring to get help from therapists or psychologists who may focus on what's going wrong in a person's life and often attempt to resolve and understand depression, schizophrenia, and anxiety. Rather, positive psychology focuses on happiness, optimism, and why people flourish. An experienced and trained coach who understands the professional service environment including the issues and challenges that are likely being confronted, can be of valuable assistance to a professional.

The Benefits to Your Career from Enhancing Your Wellbeing

Practicing and working on the core components of positive psychology is important. As a recap, the positive aspects we experience when we are connected to our career and personal life (i.e. professional wellbeing) can result in the following benefits occurring:

- *Having a positive outlook on our career and life, and expressing this state of mind in our emotions and in our relationships with colleagues and clients.*
- *Being authentically engaged in deepening relationships with our colleagues and clients as well as with friends, and family.*
- *Possessing a sense of purpose for what we set out to accomplish in our career and our work.*
- *Feeling aligned and in congruence with our strengths, talents, values, and aspirations.*
- *Maintaining a lifelong commitment to one's health that translates into a more productive and collaborative workplace.*

When put into action, enhancing your professional wellbeing can be a game changer. More than mere theory, the practice of positive psychology as it relates to your career is potent and will help you develop needed skills as part of your career development. By changing your way of thinking along with your behaviors, you can thrive.

Issues We Face in a Career that Positive Psychology Can Address

As a professional who was licensed as a Chartered Accountant in England and Certified Public Accountant (CPA) in the USA, I was trained to probe and understand in order to be able to rely on facts. The last twenty years has unfurled extensive research, many books, and a wave of progress around what makes the human condition flourish. Positive psychology has a scientific foundation that can be highly beneficial to a professional.

The fact is that the longer we practice and as we age, the more personal or career issues one may face. A few examples of the problematic issues I have witnessed professionals struggle with and can be assisted by applying positive psychology are:

- How to understand and handle burnout and fatigue. Not addressing these issues can in turn can lead to being stressed and hamper an ability to manage issues with practice partners, colleagues, or clients. Understanding and infusing self-compassion and building resilience skills can be important in addressing fatigue or burnout.
- A lack of an ability to be adept at confronting and managing conflict. Disruptive relationships can quickly become toxic relationships.
- Issues that can surface from unexpected corners due to cross-cultural communications. These can be tough issues requiring a focus on empathy to different cultures.
- When the proverbial water boils over in a relationship, we naturally can become angry. Learning how to manage emotions is important to avoid creating rifts in relationships with colleagues or clients.
- Understanding trust and how to embrace it or repair it as a cornerstone to all relationships including those with colleagues. A lack of trust can also impede the ability to delegate and manage effectively as a professional.
- As a career can span several decades, one may face midlife

challenges that can impact a mid to late stage career. Midlife issues in professionals can be common when faced with mandatory retirement or burn out. There may be a burning internal desire for a second act career, or the desire to retire, or simply to reinvent oneself. These issues may likely indicate a need to realign to work/life balance. However, often a professional suppresses or hides these desires since there may be career self-identity concerns as well as compensation needs that prevent change.

The above examples, and no doubt others, effect our emotions, focus, and ability to be present and engaged at work. These will impact performance, which ultimately will be noticed by colleagues, supervisors, and clients.

Concluding Reflections

My experience is that when professionals have the tools, training, and awareness of positive psychology to handle these types of issues or situations, it can result in enhancing a career with life changing success.

NINE
REINVENTION AND REWIREMENT

"Every man must decide whether he will walk in the light of creative altruism or in the darkness of destructive selfishness." — Martin Luther King, Jr.

Given that we are living longer, it is likely that those entering adulthood today may spend 70 to 80 years as an adult - or even longer! Have you seriously contemplated what is required financially, emotionally, and spiritually to live to 100?

As we travel across the Bridge of Decumulation and Simplicity we may likely retire or perhaps as is now far more common, rewire and reinvent ourselves to a lifestyle of choice and meet an internal desire to live a life being one's true self.

Friedrich Nietzsche (October 15, 1844–August 25, 1900), was a philosopher who believed that embracing difficulty is essential for a fulfilling life, and considered the journey of self-discovery one of the greatest and most fertile existential difficulties. In 1873, as he was approaching his thirtieth birthday, Nietzsche addressed this perennial question of how we find ourselves and bring forth our gifts in an essay titled, *Schopenhauer as Educator*, part of his *Untimely Meditations*. Nietzsche summarized that the desire to reinvent is a journey that will never occur unless the first steps are taken.

A key question that each person should answer is whether the steps you take in your life are really to retire or instead rewire and reinvent yourself? This chapter is about rewiring oneself and reinventing.

I like to think of a reinvention as a reflection of the steps that need to be taken in order to be who we truly are. This should be our authentic self. Revealing your true identity by removing the "mask" and developing the strategies, actions, and tactics to pursue our passions in order to create the lifestyle of choice. This quest ultimately becomes the journey we are likely to spend as we travel through the second half of our life crossing the Bridge of Decumulation and Simplicity.

From my personal experience, your success in reinventing is impacted by how well we have handled adverse life events prior to a reinvention. My reasoning is that the understanding of what you really desire as a lifestyle of choice often is measured against what you have experienced as adversity in your lifestyle to date. This is often adversity that no one would willingly choose such as the loss of a child, loss of a job, poor health, etc. Having suffered the depths of loss can place the desire to experience the thrill of a desired lifestyle in greater focus. Our capacity to bounce back from adversity is based upon our resilience, and this is a skill that can be learnt by applying the science of positive psychology.

We need to recognize that it is impossible to anticipate all of the issues that may arise in one's life. This does not mean that one cannot be prepared, but as they say, life is unpredictable. You cannot prevent life events arising and many are outside of your control, but you can be effective in how to confront and handle substantive adverse life events. How you handle these challenges is at the core of being resilient and in my view, it is the success in handling tough challenges that shapes how one focuses and ultimately, is successful at reinvention.

Some scientists refer to resilience as akin to an emotional muscle that can be strengthened when needed. In part, to build one's resilience involves having a positive and optimistic view of life as you reframe how you want to live your life. It also involves understanding and spotting your strengths, and then playing to those strengths. When your strengths are spotted and focused, they help build your resilience. In general, by applying positive psychology when reinventing yourself becomes one way to effectively resolve the issues arising from a self-introspection. Each person's approach to what a reinvention looks and feels like is unique so there is no one approach or answer.

The rethinking of our self-identity as well as our value systems that occur during midlife may be no less demanding than the changes that occur in early adulthood or even adolescence. As we age, we are far more likely to address being defined by who we are (our true self) and contemplate what would be a lifestyle of choice. It is often a self-introspection that leads us to act on a desire to reinvent. The desire to reinvent surfaces most likely while on the Midlife Bridge while acting on it often occurs during the passage of crossing the Bridge of Decumulation and Simplicity. Often, reinventing during midlife is harder than later in life because we have to consider the need to earn income, often at levels far higher than when we are older, such as when we are well into our sixties and seventies and income is less important and passions and purpose become more pronounced and time to pursue more available. This is perhaps why reinventing during crossing the Bridge of Decumulation and Simplicity may be easier than during crossing the Midlife Bridge.

Reinvention: A Focus on Resilience, Reliance, and Renewal

Any transition, change, or reinvention engages three character strengths. These are: resilience, reliance, and renewal.

Let us explore how reinvention embraces these three strengths.

RESILIENCE —
Undertaking a reinvention without being resilient can leave you anxious and depressed, rather than renewed and energized. As we have discovered, resilience can be learnt. Resilience has been studied extensively by psychologists. The focus of the studies is on how an individual can overcome and rebound from adverse experiences.

These adverse life events can be from a divorce, injury, loss, rejection, illness, or the personal emotional disappointment from the failure to achieve professional goals.

Resilience can be learnt and developed in the ways we can handle negative moments in our life. Psychologist Martin Seligman spent many years studying how people deal with setbacks and found that there are three ways we can create hurdles to overcoming negative life events.

The first is to believe we are personally at fault, the second is to believe that the event will impact all aspects of our life, and the third is that the setback will affect us forever. If one can view negative moments without the above three applying, it helps to cope more effectively and less prone to get you down. Personally, when my daughter died, I knew within my heart I had tried everything a father could do to save her (even getting her to the top of the list for a liver transplant, but it was too late as the cancer had spread too far).

Her passing would deeply impact me but not shake my marriage, my relationships with the rest of my family, or my capacity to work. I suppose psychologists can analyze me and tell me why, but I felt from the moment she passed that with time, the pain would heal, and the happy memories of Kate would never disappear from within me. In this respect, I feel fortunate despite the circumstances.

RELIANCE —

No reinvention occurs overnight. Sometimes, leaving poor relationships or jobs with little or no prospects can propel someone in a positive direction, but it also can mean leaving behind security and comfort. The ability to rely on others and ask for help is important during transitions. While possessing a sense of autonomy is important, having help to transition is also important. Ask addicts who recover if they could have accomplished their recovery alone? Thus, a reinvention requires a balance between being self-reliant and leaning on others. It is this combination that introduces reliance of others into the reinvention equation.

· · ·

RENEWAL —

Many people identify themselves by what they do, rather than who they are. This scenario is often true for people who have identified themselves with caring for children and later find themselves as empty nesters, or spouses who have left a long-term marriage. When a transition is beckoning, especially in midlife, the underlying yearning to be authentic plays into the internal desire to be who you are, not what you do.

This becomes an issue of self-identity. Understanding and revealing one's true self in order to be authentic, however, requires stripping away the mask that I referred to earlier in the book. Thus, for a reinvention to be successful, it is important that an individual assess their psychological flexibility to want to transition and be able to enjoy an ongoing renewal.

A Brief History of Reinvention

Reinventing your life is not a new phenomenon. There were Biblical characters, such as Jeremiah, who went through self-reinventions. Jeremiah suffered much as a prophet, but had tremendous resilience and the capacity to reinvent after setbacks. Another historical example is Giovanni Battista Belzoni who was born in 1778 and flirted with a career in the priesthood before Belzoni decided to study hydraulics instead. When that career path failed, he became a strongman due to his muscular physique. He then reinvented himself as an archeologist and is indeed known as the father of modern Egyptian archaeology. He later became one of the "most illustrious men in Europe," according to famed novelist Charles Dickens.

There are examples of many who have reinvented themselves, because it is a process as old as humankind. Sometimes it was the need to survive, other times it may have been due to financial need or perhaps, due to being exiled. These may be reinventions out of necessity and there are many examples littered throughout history. Now with longevity in our presence, many have a choice and reinventing out of choice may be a luxury compared to out of necessity. It may also be harder as there are less external pressures to reinvent, since the pressure is from within.

Internal Pressures that Cause One to Reinvent

There is a lot of literature written about the pressures faced as teenagers and the changes that occur in teens. Yet as a society, we have not until recently written about nor given enough weight to the changes that occur to us as adults, especially during midlife. Transitions, especially during midlife, is our approach to commence resolving what can be quite an intense personal struggle in coming to terms with physiological, psychological, career, and relationship challenges and pressures.

As adults, we may be confronted or even accustomed to having to make difficult choices when facing alternative solutions to challenges. Fundamentally, in my view, a self-reinvention to address internal pressures can be life changing when we can personally change our perspective as it can become an opportunity or a catalyst for accomplishing amazing personal growth, for flourishing, and thriving. It is how we flourish and thrive that is at the core of the science of positive psychology.

During a self-introspection, especially during midlife, we become aware of and accepting of our mortality. This can be thought of as frightening, but it also can be a rousing and important experience. We just need the courage to act on what should be pursued to achieve a sustained sense of happiness through a lifestyle of our own choice. To many people this can be effectively accomplished through a meaningful and planned self-reinvention while to others they may need the assistance of a professional coach. More on this in the next chapter.

A reinvention may enhance qualities within us that may include a broader perspective on life than when we were a younger adult. This can include a better capacity to understand and practice gratitude or a better ability to regulate our emotions. We also realize that in order to change, we have to address how we think, our behaviors, and our habits as those that historically have served us may not be compatible when unveiling a more authentic self.

Changing Behaviors, Thinking Patterns, and Habits

I view midlife to be about self-discovery and revealing your true self. This is about being authentic while taking the journey along the path of the second half of one's life, which is how I describe the journey across the Bridge of Decumulation and Simplicity. Often during this journey, hopefully one discovers or rediscovers a real sense of purpose, perhaps decides to pursue an encore career that possesses more meaning and adapts to a lifestyle of choice that is more fulfilling. To change however requires courage, willpower, and thus, a change of your habits, thinking patterns, and behaviors.

Changing our behaviors, habits, or our lifestyle is not easy. However, our brain has tremendous capacity to adapt and change. The science of neuroplasticity, as discussed in Chapter 2, has clearly demonstrated the capacity for us to change, whatever our age or stage of life. Teaching and learning how to rewire ourselves becomes an integral part of a reinvention. Sometimes we can learn these traits by ourselves and other times, we may need to lean on a skilled and professional coach. The good news is that our brain has an amazing capacity to rewire, so we just have to have the courage to succeed and mitigate the fear of failure in order to start a reinvention either alone or with help.

Difference Between Rewiring and Reinventing — Out of Need or by Choice?

While internal pressures may underpin a reinvention to a lifestyle that one may choose, clearly many reinvent out of necessity. Some are exiled from their country of birth or where they grew up, while some are focused to reinvent as jobs are eliminated and new skills need to be acquired. There are a myriad of reasons and many people have reinvented out of necessity not choice. As they say, "Necessity is the mother of invention." During times of need, our financial survival becomes the key driver and external pressures to earn an income leads to our reinvention, not internal pressures focused on a lifestyle of choice.

There are times when the reasons to reinvent may be a combination of necessity and choice. Sounds like an interesting conundrum? An example is an executive faced with mandatory retirement. Does this impending "Damocles sword" (i.e. being required to retire) create a trigger to reinvent out of necessity or choice? How you view this opportunity can negatively or positively impact your wellbeing. A mandatory retirement may occur at the latter stages of a career when the time left is too short to earn needed income, perhaps while children are still going through college. This may force the impacted individual to have to find another job, to reinvent perhaps, but not retire. The decision making process to address this issue may be a competition between the internal desire to want to really retire or do something different, such as an encore career with less pay but more meaning. If the process is heavily influenced by your desired choices for a lifestyle you desire, your happiness is likely to be higher. This type of scenario plays out constantly throughout adulthood; however, during earlier stages of adulthood one is more likely to seek another similar paying job because there are too many years ahead and too little saved to retire or rewire to a lifestyle of choice that may result in lower income.

However, as we age and generally when we reach our 60s and 70s, our awareness of our life timeline is such that we may have saved enough to be able to retire or rewire and seek an encore career. This is likely when a reinvention to a lifestyle of choice most often occurs, during the Bridge of Decumulation and Simplicity, but there are plenty of times during adulthood when one may reinvent out of need.

The Notion of Rewiring Oneself

Is the word retirement appropriate for many in today's society? Perhaps the verb "to rewire" is a more apt term than "to retire" to describe the steps need to be taken to be prepared for second acts and encore careers. If necessity drives a need to find another job, reinventing oneself in another career may require being able to adapt and learn new skills, which are important to being successful. However, often the necessity is to have a job to earn the income to support the family. When it comes to a scenario where you have a choice to create a lifestyle of choice, a situation you have been contemplating since midlife when you may become more introspective, you need to change the way you think, act, and behave to power down to an encore career and a lifestyle that may have more time available and fun in work than earlier in adulthood. To enjoy this period of your life while crossing the Bridge of Decumulation and Simplicity requires a mindset to shed what you don't need, don't want, and don't like and focus on what you do, as a core part of enhancing your own wellbeing and achieving sustained happiness.

Thus, "to rewire" is a nod to the science of neuroplasticity. The evidence is clear that at any age rewiring our brain is feasible in order to change habits and behaviors needed to adapt to a new chosen lifestyle. Retirement used to be thought of as giving up work or our active passions in favor of a sedentary life of retirement. No more, as we can be active and engaged for many decades due to our longevity and it is often the chosen path to enjoy those decades by experiencing a chosen lifestyle that enhances your happiness.

For those in the early stages of their career, our brains are often consciously focused on developing a lifestyle around a career of choice. The actions of Millennials and now Gen Z often seek a social cause as a core element of choosing a job or career and who are not afraid to switch jobs frequently to maintain a balanced lifestyle. Baby Boomers were often committed to staying with one employer for many years if possible, and placed little emphasis on social causes within the job itself and a balanced work/life was not actively sought. This may have resulted in less time being able to parent, tend to a spouse or life partner, etc. It is gratifying to see younger generations actively choose lifestyles that bring more meaning, more balance, and more fun into their lives at an earlier stage than my generation of Boomers. It seems that the requiring my generation is undergoing may be less needed in future generations since they are active in this respect far earlier and perhaps with more success. The Gen X, Millennials, and perhaps the Gen Z generation has understood early on what previous generations later realized…that money is rarely, if ever, the motivating factor for a happier lifestyle

Transitions – A Time to Reinvent?

Transitions are an important part of every stage of our life. We transition from baby to toddler to child to teenager. As adults, we continue to transition during our life and each of the three metaphorical bridges is itself a transition. Transitions may also begin and end due life events including marriage, jobs, pursuing a dream, the loss of a loved one, or perhaps physical challenges.

Change in our lives cannot take place without transition and transitions have phases. While transitions can be difficult, we can learn to make them easier. This is especially true when we seek to reinvent out of choice.

Clearly the ability to change, including your personality, habits, behaviors or lifestyle, is much easier when you possess a strong resilience as I have written about. While as we age, our bodies may be less physically resilient, our minds may be trained to be more so, more capable of coping with change. Within our personality we may seek change in certain traits to handle a transition. The key five areas of traits are our capacity to be more extravert, more open, more stable with our emotions, more agreeable, and more conscientious. The bottom line is that it is never too late to change in order to live a happier life.

Any transition often begins with a desire or need to change. To change, we need to start by letting go of something we believed in, assumed or viewed within ourselves, or possessed an attitude about. In a sense, we say goodbye to some part of ourselves. However, without a focus on where to head to, life can become aimless.

Concluding Reflections

Most reinventions start with a life event. Those life events are often a loss that becomes the trigger that causes a self-introspection that leads to change. This introspection may ponder deep questions, but if answers are not found, a vision of your desired lifestyle, together with the strategies and action steps needed are not clearly defined. In this case, a reinvention is hard to accomplish.

We have all probably known people who want to give up some part of their life without clarity of "what's next." This approach commences a journey across a metaphorical bridge without a vision of the next stage of life or how to get there. Having a vision, clarity, and knowing where to head is important in career choice, retiring, or reinventing yourself. This is the impetus of why I developed a professional coaching model that is discussed in the next chapter to address how to reinvent oneself once you have determined that you need to seek answers to a midlife self-introspection and have asked yourself, "What's next?"

TEN

HOW TO REINVENT - A
PROFESSIONAL COACHING MODEL

U tilizing a professional coach can valuably assist anyone who seeks to apply the science of positive psychology in order to embrace the benefits. Since being happier is the quest, enhancing your wellbeing requires work; it is not a spectator sport.

The professional coaching model I have developed was the outcrop of my own experiences while working with clients and my academic work for my doctorate.

As we navigate each of the three metaphorical bridges described in earlier chapters, we are continually adapting ourselves to life and life's events. However, when a major life event does hit us, and it is usually a personal loss of some kind, there may be a deep self-introspection that can result in the desire or need to transition through a reinvention.

The self-introspection to reinvent is more likely to occur while navigating the Midlife Bridge than the Bridge of Accumulating Responsibilities or the Bridge of Decumulation and Simplicity, just simply because the Midlife Bridge is often the most internally and self-focused journey during our adulthood. Midlife is also a stage of our life when we have lived enough years as an adult to understand who we are, what we want to be, and come to realize, recognize, and understand the physiological, interpersonal, and intrapersonal challenges we may be succumbing to. The Bridge of Decumulation and Simplicity is likely the bridge when we live out executing our journey closer to our lifestyle of choice.

There are many self-help books on the market that address the "why" or "when" to rewire and reinvent. My view is that many of these books do not address "how" to reinvent.

Based on my research with psychologists, gerontologists, social scientists, and economists, as well as a compilation of interviews from my private coaching practice, I developed a coaching model based upon an approach that I call the "P Curve".

The "P Curve"

The approach of the "P Curve" is to embrace the science of positive psychology and to assist someone who wants to rewire and reinvent their life, especially if it is towards a lifestyle of choice. My professional coaching model strives to help people transition toward a happier and more satisfying life.

Underlying the phases of the P Curve is infusion of positive psychology to enhance one's wellbeing to thrive. Yet, accomplishing change requires more than just an understanding of how enhancing your wellbeing may bring sustained happiness. It involves the creation and affirmation of a vision and the development and deployment of strategies, action steps, and tactics.

My "P Curve" model is comprised of three phases that include:

- *Phase 1 - Problem identification and understanding*
- *Phase 2 - Pursuit of passions, a sense of purpose, and pleasure*
- *Phase 3 - Plan of action*

Phase 1 is focused on active listening to current issues and stresses and a client's sense of a lack of happiness as well as introducing the science of positive psychology and its benefits. Phase 2 expands as to how to apply the science to enhance their wellbeing. Phase 3 is about execution and creating a lifestyle of choice.

Let us look at each phase in greater detail.

Phase 1- Problem Identification and Understanding

If you do not understand a problem, you cannot determine if a possible answer could cure it.

What is triggering you to consider reinventing yourself? Why did this trigger occur and when? These are a few of the key questions that need answers. I often find that within the answers is valuable information that will likely reveal stress points and the root cause for a self – introspection as it is important to understand as much as possible about the stress points and triggers that may be causing you to ask, "What's next?"

During this phase of my coaching model, I conduct a detailed intake assessment, probing and eliciting as much as I can through active listening. In this way, a client can relate to his or her life event(s) as the trigger(s) to questions that are causing concern and framing their issues with the perspective of the present happiness of their own life. More than likely, biological, psychological, and interpersonal forces are entwined to make one step back and re-evaluate life and to address the physiological, interpersonal, and intrapersonal challenges faced. This process in Phase 1 may help a client understand why for example, a job loss, children leaving home, or a health scare may be the trigger to a self-introspection.

The objective in Phase 1 is to not delve back into issues that have arisen in the person's life, but rather, to educate a client where they are in their present stage of adulthood, why they may be experiencing an introspection of their life and frame how they can improve their well-being and thrive going forward.

Phase 2 - Pursuit of Passions and a Sense of Purpose and Pleasure

It may sound simplistic to do but hard to execute when I ask a client if they can summarize in thirty words or less what brings them pleasure, what provides them a sense of purpose, and what they are passionate about? I have found that defining the answers has not been easy for many clients.

I do believe that the ability to understand and focus on living your passions results in experiencing heightened senses of pleasure and purpose, which is key to your overall happiness. Not everyone has clearly defined passions. Therefore, developing clarity over them is critical to moving forward as pursuing your passions will likely intensify the ability to have a greater sense of purpose and experience pleasure.

Bringing greater meaning or purpose into your life should include grasping a greater awareness of being present and engaged in all that you do, becoming more altruistic, showing greater empathy and compassion, practicing mindfulness through becoming more spiritual and practicing gratitude on a daily basis. All of these attributes are important in positive psychology and each can and often do play an important role in experiencing a greater sense of purpose.

What may inspire us in the first half of our life might likely cease to have the same impact to us in the second half of our life. For example, the attraction of acquiring "toys" while traversing the Bridge of Accumulating Responsibilities is reversed during our crossing of the Bridge of Decumulation and Simplicity as they are shed due to having less meaning to us. As another illustration, our desire to be more spiritual and feel a constant sense of purpose, however, is in reverse, gaining in importance and focus during the third bridge.

To understand your passions better and what might provide you a greater sense of purpose and increased pleasure, please consider the following questions, none of which are necessarily easy to answer.

- *What pursuits are you good at?*
- *What excites you?*
- *What difference do you wish to make?*
- *Why do you get up in the morning?*
- *How do you stay on purpose?*
- *How do you live longer and better?*
- *What do you feel is the meaning of life?*
- *What energizes you?*

By answering these or other questions you can gain a sense in

Phase 2 of the importance of passions, purpose, and pleasure. You are also hopefully more prepared and ready to tackle addressing your approach as to how to reinvent.

Phase 3 - Executing a Plan of Action

In this, the third phase stage of the P Curve, the focus is on the development and execution of a plan of action to achieve your lifestyle of choice.

All of the following steps are critical and include creating a vision for your future lifestyle, visualizing your goals, committing all of this to paper, developing strategies to achieve the vision, and having tactics and action steps to get there. When thought through, defined and put into written form, you then may have a plan to achieve your lifestyle of choice and you can go for it.

Creating a Vision for Your Future Lifestyle

If you desire reinvention, then it should not all be about the end game, but rather the journey and how you can obtain sustained happiness during that journey. Since creating a vision for your chosen lifestyle is neither necessarily easy to undertake nor accomplish, embracing and enjoying your journey is very important and you should not lose sight of this.

So how do you define your vision not just for your personal life, but also for the world around you? Defining or redefining your vision is the important first step when you realign what you want your achievements and accomplishments to be during the second half of your life. In this way, you can plan for this part of your journey to feel positive and permit you to thrive while acknowledging that you want to move toward a happier and more fulfilled life.

As you proceed, you may question how you define success during this journey? Hopefully, you may define success as being happy on a sustained basis. Most will likely agree that success is not solely defined in monetary terms. Autonomy is often a critical driver in the creation of your chosen lifestyle. In other words, to be in control of your own life. Taking responsibility for your own life extends to your ability to create a powerful, personal vision of your desired future.

Instead of feeling that you have unconsciously reacted as you moved through earlier stages of your adulthood, now you can own a consciously chosen outcome. This written vision statement begins with what you want to be, followed by what you want to do and then what you want the results of your actions to be. Best yet, generating a clear vision is a natural, human skill, which can be learned.

One popular technique for goal obtainment is by creating a vision board with photo images of one's desires. Another unconventional visioning coaching technique is to pen your own obituary. Such an exercise permits you to state the importance of your life story as it will require focus. You would want to focus on (a) resolve, (b) perspective, (c) accuracy, and (d) acceptance and connection. In using this technique, you need to be unbiased and identify the gaps between today and the future as your obituary should reflect your desired lifestyle of choice.

My preference is that your visualization should be documented by a concise, written description and then shared with trusted people for input before being placed into action. I like to use a two-prong approach in working with clients on their vision. I ask clients to describe the vision of their desired lifestyle in both 30 months from when they start this visioning and also 30 years in the future. This is not an easy request, especially when I ask the client to summarize their thoughts into two written visions, each of less than 300 words, for 30 months and 30 years out. However, the output is revealing and dynamic and worth the time and effort for clarity and acceptance as it is often shaped with input from close friends and family.

Developing Strategies, Goals, and Action Steps

Once you have a clear vision and you have committed it to writing, then your goals, strategies, and action steps need to be developed and prioritized. Strategies, goals, and action steps are different from visions, hopes, wishes, and dreams. Achieving your vision is more than memorializing the vision, as it requires goals, strategies and action steps. Therefore, to achieve your vision, you must have a plan. Formulating a strategy is how we implement our plan. A clear and well developed strategy saves time, effort, and money. Without our initial vision, goals and plans are relatively useless.

Your plan should include both short and long-term goals and strategies. Even though you have committed a plan to paper, it can be challenged and will constantly need to be updated and revised, but because it is written, it also becomes easier to communicate and understand. Goals and strategies should flow after the vision has been created. Having personal goals cannot be overemphasized. For example, it is important to define the actions needed and who is going to do the work to attain the results. A clear plan of action is therefore the first and highly obtainable step after having developed the written summary of your vision of the desired choice of lifestyle. In developing your plan of action, it is important to listen to your inner voice that speaks to you about your passions and what provides you a meaningful sense of pleasure and purpose. Find supportive friends, family members, and community members to affirm what you seek if obtaining their input is of value to you. Most importantly, don't discount your goals or plans.

Of course, no two strategies are identical in developing a plan to achieve a vision. Patrick Williams and Lloyd J. Thomas in their book, *Total Life Coaching: A Compendium of Resources: 50+ Life Lessons, Skills, and Techniques to Enhance Your Practice...and Your Life,* developed the following tips for designing strategies:

- *Determine the personal and situational constraints that are involved with your plan. Can these constraints be limited?*
- *Does your current lifestyle and strategies address the constraints?*
- *Have you talked to others with similar strategies, especially those who have accomplished their goals?*
- *Identify people who already possess skills that will help you to implement your strategy.*
- *Identify your own core competencies and strengths that will help you to execute your strategies.*

- *Ask others around you to present ideas that might enhance your strategies.*
- *Consider strategies from the point of view of an outsider to gain a fresh perspective.*
- *Communicate your strategic action plan to those affected by its execution. For that matter, communicate regularly with everyone involved in the implementation of the strategy and make changes based upon feedback.*
- *Recognize and reward everyone who has helped in the implementation of your strategies.*

The art of a good professional coach is to assist the client to develop their vision and their plan of action, to have it all written down so it is memorialized and be capable of being monitored and updated. The key is that it is the clients' plan not that of a coach.

Possessing Willpower to Overcome the Fear of Failure

Thinking through and developing a written goal or strategy sounds easy enough, so why are so many people hesitant to put this into action? Many are likely hesitant to take action perhaps without being fully aware of their own fear of failure of not achieving the goal. Just as we may check the weather or road conditions before venturing out on a long car ride where weather or traffic conditions could impede a journey, so should we be aware that setbacks might occur in a reinvention, but this should not stop us from taking our journey. Many however who contemplate a reinvention intimately fear failure and thus, never pursue the steps required.

Stephen L. Antczak wrote in Next Avenue magazine in 2015 about *5 Ways to Think about Failure in Midlife.*" His essay focused on a career or business failure, positing that the same principles apply to a midlife reinvention and fear of failure. He proposed five ways to think about failure when approaching a reinvention:

1. *Failure is something that happens, not something a person becomes.*

2. *If your significant other or child had a chance to take a risk and failed, would you consider them a failure or admire them for having taken the risk?*

3. *Failure can be a valuable experience. Ask anyone who has the resilience to bounce back.*

4. *Life is too short to dwell on past failures, even recent ones.*

5. *Since failure later in life is harder to recover from than when we're young, it is important to think about it in a way that propels us to take necessary steps to push forward.*

I believe that there are at least two important attributes that are important to any reinvention and can counter fear of failure. These are the mindset to reinvent and having the willpower to go through it. If you have a fixed mindset, then you might assume that to change, transition, or reinvent will indeed be a radical change because there is no capacity to think beyond the current state of lifestyle. A growth mindset is always preferred and is important in order to create the vision and desire to change or reinvent.

Even if you possesses a growth mindset to reinvent, fear of failure or inertia may prevent you from accomplishing it. So, possessing the willpower to change is another necessary component.

Willpower is about self-control. *Willpower: Rediscovering the Greatest Human Strength,* written by Roy F. Baumeister and John Tierney, discusses how willpower lets us change ourselves as well as society. In their book, they commented that the first step in self-control is to set a goal. Importantly and ultimately, self-control lets you relax because it removes stress and enables you to conserve willpower for the important challenges. Practical wisdom and scientific research makes it clear that we need to harness self-control to reach our goals, which should be realistic. While a more detailed discussion is beyond my book, focusing our strengths, being able to resist temptations and redirect our lives are important in our self-control to have the willpower to reinvent.

Challenging Questions to Ask Ourselves

There are, in my view, important questions we face during each of the three bridges of adulthood. Each metaphorical bridge poses questions that helps you focus your thoughts toward your values, goals, and aspirations. When answered authentically, the questions and subsequent thought processes that results will lead you to thrive in your life

Here are some probing and perhaps challenging questions I often pose to my clients while coaching. These questions can produce thought provoking impact in how and why applying the science of positive psychology can be used to enhance one's wellbeing:

WHAT REALLY MATTERS TO YOU?

Consider what matters to you as well as whether a greater focus on happiness and wellbeing might be better, not just for yourself, but for everyone around you. This question also considers whether sustained happiness can and should be thought of as the ultimate good for society.

WHAT MAKES YOU HAPPY AND WHY SHOULD SUBJECTIVE WELLBEING BE important to you?

Happiness is subjective, but it can be measured in a reliable and meaningful way as has been described earlier. The subjective results are meaningful because they correspond with objective measurements such as responses of our immune system and how they correlate with brain activity, specifically with positive emotional states linked to the left side of the pre-frontal cortex and negative emotions linked to the right side.

CAN YOU FIND PEACE OF MIND BY CHOOSING AND CREATING A LIFESTYLE OF your choice?

Having peace of mind in a stressful world is about mindfulness, which is choosing to pay attention to what is happening in the present moment. It involves having conscious awareness of your current thoughts, feelings, and surroundings, but also adapting to an attitude of curiosity, openness, and acceptance to whatever arises in the moment. While mindfulness was inspired by Eastern teachings and Buddhist traditions, it is not religious in nature.

Are you consciously aware?

Life is stressful, and often a life event that triggers an introspection can intensify stress. Triggers may originate from work, financial, or relationship issues can create feelings of loneliness, pressure, or being overwhelmed. Developing resiliency through peace of mind helps you feel in control of your own destiny. Being consciously aware means practicing mindfulness to see what is in front of us and then perhaps, letting these issues go and instead, focusing on what we can control. Mindfulness has profound, positive effects on our brains and our health, while influencing how we function with our family, at work, and in the world.

How should you be engaged in treating others?

Developing and maintaining strong relationships is a key element of positive psychology. Deeply positive relationships involve emotional and social intelligence. This includes the need to have skills in awareness and management of your own emotions, the emotions of others, and appropriate behaviors needed for social interactions. For many years, intelligence (often referred to as IQ) was the most important factor for success in life and work. Today, effectively using emotions and relating to others is considered to have a substantial impact as well. Unlike IQ, emotional and social intelligence can be learned and improved upon.

These next questions are inter-related.

- Can you be happier at what you do?
- Can you help to create a happier world?

- Should your community and beyond care about your happiness as well as that of the community?
- Can you define what would bring you peace of mind and create a lifestyle of your choice to help a wider community beyond yourself?
- What constitutes a great relationship for you?

The capacity, desire, and ability to connect is at the cornerstone of humankind. Some of us have stronger interpersonal skills than others, yet this does not mean that those who have less have not developed skills in this area, nor the desire to connect. It is important to distinguish between meaningful versus superficial relationships because the former are where a great relationship can reside.

A great relationship is built upon the development of trust, vulnerability, the desire to share, and the lack of fear of reprisal. Having authentic relationships are critical to each of us. Great and meaningful relationships are what we wish for as parents with our children, with our spouses or significant others as well as with our parents and true friends. Of course, our desires are not always achieved, and relationships can come unstuck and this can be painful, since the desire to inflict pain or hurt has not stopped humankind to seek deep relationships while simultaneously possessing the capacity to harm, inflict damage and treat fellow humankind in anything like a positive or great relationship.

Concluding Thoughts about Undertaking a Reinvention - It's Possible!

Reinvention is neither straightforward, easy, nor simple. Yet, it can be illuminating and rewarding and lead one to an enhanced state of well-being. This can lead to sustained happiness by opening your mind, by encouraging a growth mindset, embracing and understanding stress, and encouraging you to have the willpower to change.

ELEVEN

HOW TO OVERCOME SPECIFIC CHALLENGES FACED IN ADULTHOOD

Human Development is about expanding the richness of human life rather than simply the richness of the economy in which we human beings live. Human Development is about an approach that is focused on people, their opportunities, and choices. I have always found this to be a fascinating topic and my passion resulted in my pursuit of a doctorate in this field.

My passion also propelled me to explore the research behind the science of positive psychology since the research has proven how humans can flourish or thrive. Fortunately, we can all enjoy the benefits of enhancing our wellbeing, regardless of our age, gender, race, religion, nationality, or societal background.

As the field of positive psychology has developed over the past 20 years or so, so too has coaching matured into a profession. Having completed my masters and doctorate degrees in both professional coaching and human development, practiced as a coach, and advised and consulted for decades, I found that studying the cutting edge of positive psychology can provide fundamental value to the field of human development. I am convinced that the intersection of human development, positive psychology, and professional coaching has a clear role and bright future in assisting people to flourish and thrive.

While enhancing wellbeing is the journey to capture the benefits from thriving, one's personal development is a continuous and lifelong effort.

Reality is that as we travel across my three metaphorical bridges, there will be common challenges that may impede your wellbeing. These challenges may include stress, burnout, negative emotions, a lack of trust, nefarious motives, inappropriate goals, identity issues, and conflicts among many. How many of these have you experienced? Likely a lot.

Positive psychology and professional coaching can assist in managing these challenges.

I found that understanding myself has helped me. The Oracle at Delphi in 1,400 BC said, *"Know Thyself."* It is as true today over 3,000 years later. I have used the Myers-Briggs Type Indicator test (MBTI), various strengths testing tools, and the Thomas-Killman conflict mode tool for clients to better understand themselves and others.

The MBTI approach focuses on four components focused on:

- *How do you like to energize? Extraverts or Introverts*
- *What information do you trust? Sensors or Intuitives*
- *How do you prefer to make decisions? Thinkers or Feelers*
- *What type of lifestyle suits you best? Judgers or Perceivers*

The 16 possible personalities each display strengths and personalities, and reveals your temperament. Temperament is a kind of fingerprint and a simplified way of understanding complex behaviors. It allows us to appreciate differences between individuals and is a combination of the information we trust and how we use that information in the world. The result are four types of temperament: an Artisan, Guardian, Rational, and Idealist. There are many excellent books that cover this in more detail and worth reading. One I have kept close to me for around 30 years is *Please Understand Me: Character and Temperament Types* by David Keirsey and Marilyn Bates. There is much to glean and appreciate from understanding personality types and temperaments, which is beyond the scope of this book. However, there are clear implications of why you may be under stress since Carl Jung (upon whose work Myers Briggs is based) identified your inferior function, which develops last as an adult and comes out as shadow behavior when under stress. The dominant function develops first, then auxiliary, tertiary, and finally, the inferior function. Once all of this is understood there are ways to deal with shadow behaviors.

Since our journey throughout adulthood is littered with obstacles, I thought it would be beneficial to highlight some specific challenges.

Addressing specific challenges faced in adulthood

Let us take a light and shine it on certain challenges we may face and reflect how to look at each challenge:

- *Stress - Why not all stress is bad and how to handle it*
- *Burnout - How to recognize the symptoms and overcome it*
- *Emotions - The interpersonal, intrapersonal, and social/cultural function of emotions and how to manage them*
- *Trust - The importance to building and deepening relationships*
- *Motives and Goals - How willpower and courage is relevant to achieving them*
- *Legacy - One's sense of meaning and the search for purpose*

Stress — Why not all stress is bad and how to handle it

Research has proven that the science of positive psychology focuses on what contributes to human happiness and emotional health. Yet everyone feels stress at some time during their life. Many believe that stress can only be bad. However, in reality there is both good and bad stress. Understanding the difference is critical to how you react and handle stress; and thus, how you possess the appropriate viewpoint that can positively impact the quality of your life.

Bad stress can be thought of as distress and can hinder everyday life, prevent you from completing tasks, and if not relieved can be detrimental to your health. Elevated levels of stress hormones like cortisol and adrenaline are perhaps acceptable in the short run and come into play in a fight or flight situation, but in the long run, they lead to weakened adrenals. The body's immune system becomes compromised and this can lead to depression, weight gain, heart disease and memory loss, which none of us seek. Probably, we all have been in a bad stress situation if we have ever lost a close friend or family member. You can alleviate distress by breathing, meditating, undertaking physical exercise or compartmentalizing the stress to manage it better. Chronic stress and elevated cortisol levels can unfortunately lead to an increased risk of depression.

Good stress, is also known as eustress. If someone believes that all stress is bad, the outcome is not good. So being able to understand and recognize good stress is important. Good stress may be a mild stress and rather than being harmful, can enhance and improve your cognitive brain function. For example, feeling stressed before giving a big speech or taking a major test is good stress, since the stress helps with clarity and creativity. Eustress occurs during the excitement faced with overcoming an obstacle. This compares with distress, which does not provide the feeling of wellbeing and relief directly afterwards, because distress propels an individual into a downward cycle that wears down the mind and body.

In eustress "good stress," dopamine floods the brain, which stimulates creativity and focus. Dopamine, like norepinephrine, is a neurotransmitter in the brain that initiates adrenaline, a hormone that is activated during the stress response.

Stress response is normally self-regulating such as when you experience constant stress, your stress response system is continually on. This can create a dangerous and potentially threatening condition for the body as this process floods the body with excess hormones, raises your blood pressure, and elevates blood sugar levels, creating a host of physical and psychological problems as dopamine rules your motivational forces and your psychomotor speed in the central nervous system.

For example, during a sports event, the role of dopamine and the stress response trigger is initiated to get the physical and mental sports challenge accomplished and then returns to your baseline. This is the same process that occurs when faced with a big speech, major test, or some other good stress situation. By contrast, strains from financial issues, abusive relationships and other prolonged, negative events can overwork the stress response system and become a drain on the body. This is bad stress. Excess stress can deplete your dopamine stores, which has a ripple effect on nearby endorphins, which are necessary to prevent pain and maintain a good mood. Chronic stress and the depletion of dopamine is an environment that can enable Alzheimer's, Parkinson's, heart disease, cancer, and other auto immune disorders to unfortunately arise.

Distinguishing between good and bad stress is often difficult when you are under stress. For the reasons I have outlined, it is important to determine what kind of stress we are under. If we end up being invigorated it is probably good stress, whereas if we end up tired and unenthusiastic it is likely bad stress.

POSITIVE PSYCHOLOGY, SO FAR AS IT RELATES TO STRESS MANAGEMENT, has identified several positive emotional stress states that can contribute to greater emotional resilience, health, and happiness. Examples are:

- *Gratitude - The ability to appreciate what you have, which can lead to a sense of gratitude and lift your mood.*
- *Optimism - A tendency towards being optimistic in your outlook and the benefits derived from thinking this way can also counter stress.*
- *Flow - Being absorbed/engaged while being in your " zone" can also assist in mitigating stress. I like to think that as a runner and cyclist for many years, when I exercise, I am totally focused on what I am doing and by shutting out the issues of the hour, I am more capable of handling stress. I know I am not alone on this, which is why so many who exercise benefit so immensely not just from a physical health aspect, but also mentally.*
- *Mindfulness – Similar to being in the zone, one of the core positive*

psychology elements known as "flow," by being fully present in the
"now" can bring benefits and mitigate stress.

- *Spirituality - This can lead to a greater sense of meaning and*
  resilience in the face of stress. Prayer and meditation can make you
  more centered and be supportive to stress management.

TRY THIS THREE-PART COACHING INTERVENTION, USED AS A POSITIVE psychology tool, to mitigate stress:

1. *Identify the Stressful Situation: "I am stressed about...?"*
2. *Ask: "What do I really care about in this situation?*
3. *Consider: How can I view/use my response to this stress as a*
   resource? (i.e. How can I use the physical energy, lessons etc. of
   this situation to move me forward instead of taking me back).

Clients can be coached on how to utilize stress along with "values affirmations" to remind us of our inner resources and help us choose how we respond and manage stress. Aligning stress to our values is also important because our values become our moral compass, thus providing us direction to solutions when faced with an issue. This roadmap can lower our stress levels. Often, it is the inability to figure out a solution to a problem that increases your stress level.

Although stress is a common problem that can be harmful and debilitating, we should take comfort in knowing that there are solutions to understanding and mitigating it.

Burnout - How to recognize the symptoms and overcome burnout

Ask almost anyone and they no doubt have probably experienced times when they felt tired after a full day, week or month of work. Sooner or later, they will feel a need for a vacation. However, when you feel exhausted all the time, marked perhaps by a lack enthusiasm at work or with colleagues, you can become cynical and disengaged and likely are exhibiting symptoms of burnout. Unfortunately, as we become busier and our lives become more demanding, such as when you are crossing the Bridge of Accumulating Responsibilities, everything can become more stressful, resulting in burnout.

Burnout was a term developed in the 1970s by Dr. Herbert Freudenberger, a psychologist who specialized in burnout. He co-authored a definitive book on burnout along with Geraldine Richelson called, *Burn Out: The High Cost of High Achievement - What It Is and How To Survive It.* Freudenberger offered this analogy of a burned-out house:

"If you have ever seen a building that has burned out, you know it's a devastating sight...some bricks or concrete may be left; some outline of windows. Indeed, the outer shell may seem almost intact. Only if you venture inside will you be struck by the full force of the desolation."

So, it is quite likely that someone who is burnt out may not seem that way from the outside, but internally they are as if "on fire," with a great void within.

THERE ARE THREE PARTS TO BURNOUT:

- *Exhaustion – Being exhausted can make one upset, marked by having trouble sleeping, being more prone to becoming sick, and exhibiting problems of being able to concentrate.*
- *Cynicism - Also called depersonalization, with a feeling of being alienated from your colleagues and lacking in engagement at work.*
- *Inefficacy - A lack of belief in yourself and your ability to perform the job well and a decrease in your achievement and productivity.*

Being burnt out is not about overworking too hard or for too long a time, but rather it is the outcome when the balance of deadlines, demands, hours and other stress points outstrip rewards, recognition, and relaxation.

For example, when I analyze a client's dissatisfaction with the current status of their career, I look at areas such as workload, the client's control over their work or lack of it, how much autonomy they are missing in their life, the actual rewards versus what is desired, how connected they are with a community, and how a client vies their current status as fair and aligned with their values. If the majority of these seem out of balance, then it can be signals that can lead to burnout.

Burnout effects your brain as well as your body. For the brain, it can result in an impairment of memory, lack of attention, and emotional issues. For the body, it can increase heart disease.

So how can you overcome burnout? You can start by managing your workload perhaps by delegating more and learning to say no, which in itself is not necessarily easy to do. How many of us know we should eat well, stay hydrated, sleep well and exercise, but don't change the way we live our daily life even when we suspect we are heading towards burnout, until it is too late? Sometimes for an individual sensing burnout, it is as much a matter of discovering a remedy that works as the remedy itself. It can be as simple as listening to or attending to the needs of your inner self as opposed to the outside world.

Challenging and changing our internalized habits of working to improve productive time allocations prompts one to think about how to adjust your lifestyle to a life worth living, rather than the lifestyle one is in.

Emotions - Interpersonal and Intrapersonal

There are social and cultural aspects of emotions that we need to learn to manage. Our emotions play a crucial role in our lives. Simply put, they have an important function as they are a vital aspect of our physiological composition, providing meaning and function to ourselves and our relations with others and within society. Emotions provide experiences that infuse taste, vibrancy, and vivid colors into our lives.

For over a hundred years, emotions have been the focus of scientific research. So why are emotions important and why do we even have them?

One way to look at emotions is to first look at the *intrapersonal* functions of emotions and how they play out within each of us. Next is to address the *interpersonal* functions which relate to the emotions of individuals within a group. Last are the *social and cultural functions* which relate to the role of emotions in maintaining structure and order within a community or society.

Intrapersonal Functions

There are four main reasons why emotions help an individual relating to your internal intrapersonal functions.

1. Emotions enable you to act quickly with minimal conscious awareness. This is important when making decisions about whether to, for example, attack, defend, flee, care for others, reject food, etc. These types of emotions have been adapted over time and are required to survive without any depth of thinking. They are, for example, the emotions that kick in you are faced with imminent danger.

2. Emotions prepare an individual's body for immediate action and orchestrate how we function in areas such as perception, attention, inference, learning, memory, goal choice, motivational priorities, physiological reactions, motor behaviors, and behavioral decision making. Emotions also simultaneously activate certain systems and deactivate others to prevent chaos of competing systems and allow for coordinated responses to stimuli in our environment.

3. Emotions influence our thoughts. Our memories are colored with the emotions felt when events have occurred. Thus, emotions serve as the connectors in our brain. Some have called this the neural glue that connects disparate facts in our minds and hence, the reason to remember happy

thoughts when happy and angry thoughts when angry. They serve as the basis of many attitudes, values, and beliefs. Emotions give statements meaning and influence our thinking processes. It is difficult to think critically when we feel intense emotions, but easier to think critically when we are not overwhelmed with emotions.

4. Emotions motivate our future behaviors. As emotions prepare our body for immediate action, they influence our thoughts and can be felt. We strive to experience positive emotions, but work hard to avoid repeating emotions of disgust by taking actions to ensure the situation does not repeat itself.

INTERPERSONAL FUNCTIONS

There are three main reasons why our emotional expressions facilitate how we interact with one another, which are our interpersonal emotions:

1. Our emotional expressions facilitate specific behaviors in how they are perceived through the verbal and non-verbal emotions we emit (e.g. our voice, body postures, gestures, and movements). These emotional expressions are constantly expressed when interacting with others. Others can reliably judge these emotional expressions and they possess value as they have an influence on others in our social interactions. Thus, emotions and expressions communicate information about our feelings, intentions, and relationship with the recipient of our emotions. This, in turn, produces behaviors from the recipient who is our target and the perceiver of the emotions we are emitting.

2. Our emotional expressions also signal the nature of our interpersonal relationships. Based upon detailed research of married couples, examples between marital partners of discrete expressions of contempt by men and disgust by

women predicted marital dissatisfaction and even divorce. The point to be noted is that emotional expressions provide information about the nature of our relationships.

3. Our emotional expressions also provide incentives for our desired social behaviors. Emotions can help solve social problems by evoking responses, signaling the nature of interpersonal relationships and by providing incentives for desired, social behavior. The facial expressions we make are social signals throughout the world. They express meaning about our intent and our subsequent behavior as well as our psychological state. This impacts what the perceiver of our emotional expression is likely to do.

SOCIAL AND CULTURAL FUNCTIONS

Most of us would agree that humankind and the world we live in is complex. There are a multiple of groups we are members of, and even multiple cities we may live, vacation in or visit during our lives. There are also multiple expectations as we move in and out of many groups probably many times throughout adulthood.

Culture provides coordination and organization for us to negotiate our social life with some semblance of order and with the absence of chaos. Culture also provides a meaning and information system for its members and it is shared across generations. This permits survival and the ability to pursue happiness and enhance wellbeing.

Cultures also inform us what to do with our emotions, particularly how to manage or modify them when experienced. Culture affects how we express emotions as well as experience them. As an example, what may be acceptable in the USA may not be acceptable in Asia and vice versa.

Cultures thus create world views, rules, guidelines, and norms concerning emotions because emotions have important intra- and interpersonal functions and are important motivators of behaviors. Therefore, our emotions have a critical role to play in the successful functioning of any society and culture.

How to Generate Positive Emotions

We have seen that possessing a positive attitude pays off with bene-fits to our health and enhancing our wellbeing. The following are specific strategies to generate positive emotions:

- Hope: Creating a plan of action and a vision of our future starts out with small steps. Ggoing forward with a positive mindset may feel doable with a mindset of a scientist saying, "Let's experiment" by which you display with positive emotive emotions.
- Pride: By understanding, uncovering, and playing to your strengths and talents, you can take pride when you realize your goals and feel successful.
- Interest: Set your goals so that you can engage in them and while perhaps a stretch, they do not produce anxiety within, but instead, the goals generate positive emotions.
- Love: By fostering trust, rapport, and a connection with a person you wish to have deepened relationships with, it will create a form of social support.
- Awe: By identifying inspiring role models and heroes, you can hold them in awe and become inspirational for you.
- Amusement: Laugh at yourself and your situations so you do not take life too seriously. As they say, "Laughter is the best medicine."
- Joy: Improve your sense of awareness and enjoyment of thriving during your life journey.
- Serenity: Stop and savor moments of contentment in your life. Life is busy; we need that time to savor and express gratitude, which we will cover next.

The benefit of gratitude for positive emotions.

Possessing positive emotions should include gratitude. Expressing and feeling gratitude can create a tremendous coping mechanism. Even in grave situations, such as terrorist attacks, people can find solace through gratitude. Gratitude improves our relationships, and thus, enhances your subjective wellbeing. Gratification results when people utilize their individual strengths and virtues to do something that they personally find valuable. Furthermore, gratitude becomes a form of social glue and the thread of compassion in a society.

Research published in the *Journal of Cerebral Cortex*, found that gratitude stimulates the hypothalamus, which is the key part of the brain that regulates stress. Gratitude also stimulates the ventral tegmental area, which is part of the "reward circuitry" in our brain that produces the sensation of pleasure. Possessing an attitude of gratitude brings you better health and is tied to conscientiousness. Grateful people are found to be healthier, exercise more, eat better, and devote more time to helping others.

Trust - The importance to building and deepening relationships

Trust is the act of placing confidence in someone or something else. Trust is a fundamental human experience, necessary for society to function and for any person to be relatively happy. Without trust, fear rules. Certain life experiences can impact an ability to trust others and when trust is not present, relationships suffer.

So, what are the common signs and symptoms of trust issues? Let us start with the assumption that everyone has uncertainty about who to trust, how much to trust, or when not to trust. Every day we make decisions on questions of trust. At times, we are more willing to trust than other times. A total lack of mistrust of everyone indicates a serious psychological problem, so it is a good thing that we make trust decisions all the time, since our judgments about trust help keep one safe and alive.

Being excessively mistrustful often presents itself with signs such as:

- *A total lack of intimacy or friendships due to mistrust.*
- *Mistrust that interferes with one's primary relationship.*
- *Several intensely dramatic and stormy relationships either at the same time or sequentially.*
- *Constant thoughts of suspicion or anxiety about family and friends.*
- *Terror during physical intimacy.*
- *A belief that others are deceptive and malevolent without real evidence.*

Mistrust can play a significant role in your life, especially if past betrayals or disappointments are at the core of the issue. Mistrust is valid as a response, if for example, you have been abandoned, but this can also lead to a lack of commitment in other relationships. Your life can be adversely affected when mistrust is pervasive as it creates anger or self-doubt. Trust issues can also arise if based upon experiences and interactions in your childhood. For example, if you did not receive adequate nurturing, affection, or acceptance as a child, if as an adolescent you experienced social rejection by being treated as an outcast, or as an adult if a loved one was lost. Any of these circumstances may be issues that can impact trusting others to feel safe and secure.

Being unable to trust can destroy friendships, careers, and marriages. If you are a service professional, you may constantly be dealing with colleagues and clients, and therefore, building and deepening relationships is core to a successful practice. A lack of trust can be a major obstacle to having a successful practice, especially if you do not know how to build trust. Nearly all of the reasons why relationships fail is because a lack of loyalty, honest communication and mutuality of interest due to lack or loss of trust.

Fortunately, the good news is that one can learn to trust again. So how do you build and maintain trust in relationships?

Trust versus mistrust is a matter of building a lasting bond with another human being. Whether a professional relationship or a romantic one, the most satisfying and fulfilling connections are the ones where one can trust the other person. It is not a coincidence that positive relationships are one of the core elements in positive psychology and that a focus on trust is critical, as it is the cornerstone of all relationships.

THERE ARE FOUR CRITICAL FACTORS IN ENSURING THAT TRUST RESIDES IN A relationship:

1. Values - A common set of values and a willingness to respect those that do not overlap is essential. Shared values contribute to a mutual recognition of priorities, which reduces dissension and encourages respect of the other's values and provides teachings about one's strengths and virtues.
2. Integrity - This is comprised of honesty and consistency so that there is predictability in the relationship.
3. Mutuality - This refers to working as a team within the relationship and is critical to sustained trust due to the ability to rely on one another.
4. Commitment - Loyalty is important in the relationship so that the relationship's efforts are not in vain.

THE FOLLOWING ARE TECHNIQUES THAT CAN BE DEPLOYED TO BUILD TRUST:

- Being honest - Perhaps this is the most obvious way to maintain trust since lying, being deceitful or dishonest will tear individuals and thus, the relationships apart.
- Communicating effectively – This is one of the main reasons for failed relationships. This is an area that you can continually develop through training and practice. Empathetic listening and active, constructive communication are important in creating mutual understanding and developing trust.
- Controlling impulsive decision making - Any relationship

will have a hard time when other parties believe they are not a part of important decisions. This can occur in the workplace when supervisors take actions that impact subordinates without advising a subordinate of the likely decision before being made. Impulsive behaviors need to be tempered by self-control in decision making.

- Being reliable - Actions must match promises, otherwise it seeds distrust. As they say, "Actions speak louder than words."
- Admitting your mistakes – Making mistakes is unavoidable and failing to meet every expectation is a key part of our human experience since we are not perfect. So, confessing to mistakes and taking responsibility for your actions is important as failing to do so begs the question of what else are you concealing or lying about?
- Doing the right thing – Your moral compass can tell you whether your actions are right or wrong. Basing and using your moral compass around your values is one of the key factors in any relationship and will help others to understand, rely, and trust you. Possessing moral integrity and building a reputation on doing what is right will enhance the building of trust.
- Avoiding self-promotion - Relationships are a two-way street so it is important to respect the other person in the relationship, being grateful for their presence and the efforts they make to keep the relationship going.
- Expressing yourself - While revealing feelings may be uncomfortable and make one vulnerable, they are important in building trust. Being authentic rather than concealing true emotions can negatively impact a relationship by fostering secrecy and resentment.

Working hand in hand with trust is the capacity to express gratitude and empathy to another person. Along with trust, gratitude and empathy are foundations on which every authentic relationship and meaningful connection is built, since maintaining positive relationships is important to your wellbeing.

In summary, trust is crucial to any lasting relationship and can ebb or flow over time, so your attention to continuing to adjust and commit daily to a relationship is important to receive trust, respect, and love in return.

Motives and Goals

The decisions and behaviors we make are often the result of a goal or motive we possess. For example, come New Year many people make resolutions or goals that fairly quickly end up unfulfilled, whether it relates to exercise, diet, or improving yourself. While we may know that our lives may improve if we achieve these goals, why do so many people not follow through? Would each of us who fails to achieve our goals be better off if we accomplished them?

A goal is the cognitive representation of a desired state. It is a mental idea of how we would like things to turn out. A goal can be well-defined or abstract, such as taking a vacation to Italy versus eating healthily.

Goals that you are aware of are much more powerful than personal resolutions. Resolutions are conscious choices which depend on "will power" or "self-discipline" to fulfill. However, clear goals can generate inspiration and enthusiastic energy for you to use in the process of fulfilling them. Goals, programmed within your subconscious mind, empower you to "automatically" engage in actions, choices, thoughts, and decisions which will make goal-attainment seem effortless. Personal goals that are unfulfilled can remain desired without guilt. Resolutions are often made to relieve guilt. Goals are made to inspire and energize you to fulfill your life's desires.

Underlying these goals is our motivation. Motivation is the psychological driving force that enables our action in the pursuit of that goal and can stem from two places:

1. First, it can come from the benefits related to pursuing a goal (*intrinsic motivation*) or

2. Second, it can derive from being associated with achieving a goal (*extrinsic motivation*).

To illustrate, consider a professional service provider who is working hard on a major project. Does the professional work hard because he or she enjoys the act of learning on the job (an intrinsic motivation) or does the professional work hard because a successful project may result in a bonus or promotion (an extrinsic motivation)?

The pursuit of a goal and the motivations that underlie the goal, do not depend solely on an individual's personality. Rather, they are products of personal characteristics and situational factors. These factors can include those around us such as images, words, sounds, and people, which can activate motivations and can prime a goal. This activation can be conscious since you may be aware of the cues or it can be unconscious where you are not aware of the cues as to why you are pursuing a goal.

Behaviors are important in how we pursue goals and can be inconsistent with achieving a goal. The factors that influence a person's motivation while pursuing a goal includes self-regulation. There are factors that permit you to follow goals even when there are conflicting desires and these factors are related to self-control.

Self-regulation or self-control can be viewed as the willpower to propel you forward. As described earlier, willpower is important to committing and undertaking a reinvention to include developing a written vision and plan of action. The desire, for example, by a professional to complete a project for a client may be a self-regulated goal. This goal may conflict with the behavior of taking on too much work or interfere with that professional taking a vacation. Self-regulation refers to the process through which you alter your perceptions, feelings, and actions in the pursuit of a goal.

Self-regulation has two stages. The first phase is the deliberative stage when you decide which of perhaps many goals should be pursued during this assessment, often thought through with an open mind and a realistic mindset. The second stage is the implemental phase where your mindset is conducive to immediate action and can lead to closed-mindedness and unrealistic positive expectations about your chosen goal.

Research has shown that there are two distinct self-regulatory orientations or perceptions of effectiveness. These two orientations are prevention and promotion.

1. Prevention focuses on safety, responsibility, and security needs and views goals as "ought's" (i.e. "should be" doing goals). Self-regulation focuses on a strategy to avoid losses (e.g. losing weight after a heart attack), when the goal is something that must be accomplished to live a long life.
2. Promotion views goals as "ideals" and emphasizes hope, accomplishments, and advancements as something one wants to do rather than should do. Promotion leads to adoption of a strategy concerned with gains or positives and avoiding negatives.

An example is a perspective on saving money. Prevention focused people save because they should be doing it to avoid a scenario where they have no funds. Promotion focused people save because they want funds to do new activities that are fun. These two strategies may contain similar behaviors but with a differing focus. Self-regulation depends on feelings that arise from comparing actual progress to expected progress. During goal pursuit, a person will calculate the delta between the current and desired end states, determines the difference, and acts to close the gap.

When you have completed the steps towards achieving a goal, looking back on the behaviors or actions that assisted in progress to the goal can have implications for your future behaviors and actions. When you interpret what has occurred, you may tend to balance between the goal and other goals and put less effort into the current goal if your prior actions are viewed as progress rather than commitment, in which case you would dedicate more to the original goal. As an example, taking a course relating to your professional technical education may likely be viewed as progress and not a commitment.

There may be a tendency to take a break from education rather than power through the courses. The more you are committed to a goal, the more you may view it as progress.

In crossing any of the three metaphorical bridges there are likely to always be competing or conflicting goals, so self-control may need to be exercised to stay on course. Self-control is a process of self-regulation that can be viewed in context of involving a trade-off between long-term interests and short-term gratification. For example, a professional working on a client issue and reading relevant documents requires self-regulation while if friends or family are socializing nearby this requires self-control. The persistent capacity to postpone immediate gratification for the sake of future interests leads to greater cognitive and social competence over the course of a lifetime. However, the ability to exercise self-control can fluctuate from one area to the next as it can drain you of the limited physiological and psychological resources required to continue to pursue the goal. This is called ego-depletion.

Ego-depletion occurs when, for example, you have goals of succeeding in a career and succeeding as a spouse and parent, and self-control is required to achieve each. Eventually, you can become exhausted from pursuing both. Although resources and personal characteristics contribute to successfully exercising self-control, identifying the self-control conflict is important and often overlooked. The successful pursuit of a goal in the face of temptation requires you to identify and realize that you are having impulses that need to be controlled. The ability to identify impulses is often overlooked as an everyday temptation as it may have minimal consequence. But what if the impulses and temptations are always present and given into every day?

The protection of a valued goal involves several cognitive and behavioral strategies aimed at counteracting the pull of temptations and pushing you towards goal-related alternatives. One process involves decreasing the value of temptations and increasing the value of goal consistent objects or actions. As an illustration, we can think of being attracted to healthy fruit rather than a sugar laden cake, if weight loss is an objective. Other behavioral strategies include precommitment to pursue goals and forgo temptations. An example could be sending your family away on vacation when critical work is at hand, establishing rewards for goals, and penalties for temptations or physically approaching goals and distancing yourself from temptations.

Courage is also important in the decision to pursue goals and the motivation associated with the goal. Courage is the mental or moral strength to venture, persevere, and withstand danger, fear, or adversity. It is the strength to face opposition, hardship, and maintain dignity when it is difficult to do so.

Rabbi Zelig Pliskin described courage in his book, *Courage: Formulas, Stories and Insights,* as "the decision to transcend one's fears." A lack of courage can be a handicap, but with courage it can give you empowerment, determination, and enables you to strive towards your aspirations. Courage is a quality that enables you to speak up and act when it is difficult to do so. At times, the opposite is true, and we need courage to stay silent or refrain from acting.

Courage is also important in deciding to change your lifestyle to reinvent and then commit to act and execute upon this desire. In any reinvention journey, you need to have the courage to face adversity, strengthen your resilience to bounce back from failure, and be willing to change.

Consider how courage interplays with midlife. The first kind of courage, according to Atul Gawande author of *Being Mortal: Medicine and What Matters in the End,* is to "confront the reality of mortality." Facing mortality is often at the heart of an internal retrospection when initiated by a life event, often during midlife. The courage to seek out the truth of what is to be feared and what is to be hoped for is often at the center of facing your mortality. The courage to face mortality may be difficult enough; however, the second kind of courage is the courage to "act on the truth that is found."

Courageous acts build your character, yet courage is often only recognized after having performed such acts. Courage builds self-respect and is a state of mind. In other words, it does not have to be in effect all the time. Courage often underlines resilience in facing hardships and setbacks.

In setting your goals, you need to involve accomplishments or achievements. These may involve the pursuit of success by winning or mastery over another and often these are goals embedded into your career or life. Martin Seligman, a founder of positive psychology, argued that many people pursue an accomplishment for its own sake even when devoid of positive emotions or meaning. Seligman provided an example of players who play for the joy of the game, win or lose, whereas those who play only to win are more in pursuit of wealth than accomplishments. Billionaires who play to win and amass fortunes early in life, later on during adulthood often seek meaning by being philanthropic and giving it away.

For any goal you set, there are always motivations involved in setting accomplishments or achievements. Your goals many influence your perceptions, your feelings, and your actions of self-regulation and self-control. As we reflect on failures of previous goals, it may not seem possible to achieve some of our desires. Yet, by our own mental representation of our goals as values and expectations, we can cognitively modify our behavior to achieve our desires.

Legacy - A Sense of Meaning and the Search for Purpose

"Give me a sense of purpose, a real sense of purpose now." — Chrissie Hynde, lead singer of The Pretenders

AS EXPLAINED DURING THE CHAPTERS ON THE MIDLIFE BRIDGE AND LATER in the Bridge of Decumulation and Simplicity, as we mature, our fascination with the superficial in our lives naturally ebbs. That is why we ask deeper questions of ourselves. We probe and discover our deeper feelings through a self-introspection and seek how we can contribute to something important to our lives and in the lives of those around us.

During our midlife years, as we begin to ask questions about our purpose in life, we may also analyze our own moral compass and think through how to feel fulfillment. These questions are important as they underpin the understanding and definition of legacy. As we age, we tend to dwell on legacy with more intensity and take steps to secure our legacy. These actions usually occur in later life as we traverse the Bridge of Decumulation and Simplicity.

David Brooks, an eminent columnist with the *New York Times*, once wrote, *"Wonderful people are made, not born; they are built slowly from specific moral and spiritual accomplishments."* Brooks also wrote, *"For many people, the purpose of life is to have more life. That may not have defined people's purpose in past eras, when it might have had more to do with the next life, or obedience to a creed. But many today seek to live with hearts wide open."*

HERE IS A CRITICAL QUESTION WORTH PONDERING YOUR ANSWER TO WHEN addressing legacy — "What is your purpose?" To help you find the often elusive answer to your purpose, consider these three questions:

- What are you good at?
- What natural abilities do you possess
- What difference do you want to make?

The answers to these three questions are important to defining your sense of purpose and your legacy. My reasoning is that creating and focusing on your legacy requires understanding of your sense of purpose. Possessing a sense of purpose or meaning is important to positive psychology and thus, key to your sustained happiness.

What sets humans apart from animals is not the mere pursuit of happiness, which occurs across the natural world, but the pursuit of meaning or purpose. Meaning has a subjective component and takes on different forms to different people. But in most cases, it must meet three criteria:

1. It contributes to wellbeing;
2. It is pursued for its own sake; and,
3. Meaning can be defined and measured independent of other

elements.

My point is that focusing on one's legacy comes from clarity of what you want to accomplish and leave to the world for who you we were and what you stood for. Having clarity to your sense of purpose will better align you to the legacy you wish to create, since you leave the world the way you wanted to live your life and impact others through your passions, pleasures and most importantly, through your sense of purpose.

Legacy takes the American pursuit, "What's in it for me?" and turns it on its heel. While one may think that acquiring worldly goods will lead to happiness, the reality is that this must be tempered against the aspirations of giving back and bettering society. The universal truth is that people who lead their lives with gratitude, compassion, altruism, and a deep sense of purpose are those who find happiness and satisfaction with life satisfaction. That is not necessarily the case for those people who are measuring the material aspects of their life. This is why legacy is important.

Legacy can be viewed as the highest echelon of human aspiration, perhaps one that Abraham Maslow who wrote, *"Motivation and Personality,"* had not conceptualized about in his hierarchy of needs. Abraham Maslow's hierarchy of needs is a theory in psychology proposed in his 1943 paper, "A Theory of Human Motivation," which appeared in Psychological Review. _w_Maslow subsequently extended the idea to include his observations of humans' innate curiosity. His theories parallel many other theories of human development psychology, some of which focus on describing the stages of growth in humans. Maslow used the terms "physiological," "safety," "belonging and love," "esteem," "self-actualization," and "self-transcendence" to describe the pattern that human motivations generally move through. The goal of Maslow's Theory is to attain the sixth level or stage: self transcendent needs. Perhaps, if Maslow had considered legacy, he may have hopefully placed legacy at the top of his hierarchy of needs?

TWELVE
CONCLUDING THOUGHTS

A simple truth is that in order to find happiness and enhance your wellbeing, your pursuit of pleasures and purpose must be in balance for you since those are unique to each of us.

As we travel through our adulthood, especially during midlife, our internal thoughts will likely dwell longer and deeper about our own longevity and mortality. Upon reflection and introspection, it is feasible that we may experience regret relating to parts of our life journey and result in fear, nervousness, loss, or grief about how we may have lived our life to date. As we age, these regrets may include:

- *I wish I had the courage to live a life that is true to who I am and what I really desire, not the life others expected of me;*
- *I wish I had the courage to express my feelings;*
- *I wish I hadn't worked so hard;*
- *I wish I had stayed in touch with more of my friends;*
- *I wish I had let myself be happier during all of my journey throughout adulthood.*

Western medicine practitioners might view the feelings expressed above as symptoms and label them as pathological. However, perhaps we should look at them in a more holistic, psycho-spiritual context as these feelings may be signals that could herald a desire and need to seek a self-reinvention. A self-reinvention, however, is unlikely to occur without the firing of the trigger to ignite the desire to change so that regrets can be addressed.

The focus of positive psychology is our ability to thrive or flourish. These are not mere words, but when we strive to enhance our wellbeing, we will experience the tangible benefits.

These tangible benefits can be personally reaped for ourselves, our family, friends, colleagues, and indeed the world around us. Among these benefits are improved relationships, expressing positive emotions, a stronger sense of being engaged in all that you do and are with, improved productivity, a greater sense of meaning, collaborating more effectively, and better overall heath.

These benefits result from a science and evidence-based approach, based upon years of research relating to positive psychology as to how people and organizations thrive and excellent reasons why a reinvention, if undertaken correctly, can intensity the reaping of these benefits.

By understanding positive psychology and striving to obtain the benefits from an enhanced state of wellbeing, hopefully you can understand how positive psychology can assist you in managing challenges in your life that impact your stress, emotions, behaviors, motives, and goals. We cannot necessarily "fix" everything in our lives, but we can improve our strengths and mitigate our weaknesses. By focusing on the positives in your life instead of the negatives you can improve your happiness, health, and wellbeing. You can encourage and facilitate the positive aspects of your lives including your:

- *Wisdom and knowledge*
- *Creativity, curiosity, open-mindedness, love of learning, and perspective*
- *Courage*
- *Bravery, persistence, integrity, and vitality*
- *Humanity*
- *Love, kindness, and social intelligence*
- *Justice*

- *Citizenship, fairness, and leadership*
- *Temperance*
- *Forgiveness and mercy, humility and modesty, prudence, and self-regulation*
- *Transcendence*
- *Appreciation of beauty and excellence, gratitude, hope, humor, and spirituality*

Surely all of the above is worth pursuing and striving for?

When my daughter died, like many who have experienced a devastating event, I suspect I didn't think I could overcome my grief. Yet, it is true that life does move forward. I wanted something good to come out of her death and so, when I asked myself, "What's next," I made it a priority and one of my passions to help others who were experiencing loss, grief, challenges, change, or transition in their life.

The bottom line is that the study of human development, coupled with positive psychology, provides a strong foundation for how to accelerate human development and embrace the substantial benefits of an enhanced state of wellbeing. So ultimately, I would like to believe that as advisors, consultants, or coaches, we are solving problems relating to the human condition and assisting human development.

I hope that my book has explained and positioned adulthood into a fresh and positive context through the illustration of my three metaphorical bridges. I wish for my story and what I have covered to be of some help to dramatically improve your adult life. May you find sustained happiness both today and tomorrow as adulthood is only easy until life intervenes!

FURTHER READING

AGING —

Aging Wisely: Strategies for Baby Boomers and Seniors - Robert A Levine, MD (Rowan and Littfield, 2014)

The Big Shift: Navigating the New Stage Beyond Midlife - Marc Freeman (Public Affairs , 2011)

Disrupt Aging: A Bold New Path to Living Your Best Life at Every Age - Jo Ann Jenkins (Public Affairs. Perseus Books Group-2016)

Face It: What Women Really Feel as Their Looks Change - Vivien Diller, PhD with Jill Muir-Sukenick, Ph.D. (Hay Books, 2010)

A Fresh Map of Life: The Emergence of The Third Age - Peter Laslett (Palgrave Macmillan Publishing, 1991)

Healthy Aging - Andrew Weil, MD (Anchor Books, 2005)

Senescence: The Last Half of Life - G Stanley Hall, Ph.D. LL.D (CreateSpace Publishing, 2010)

Still Here: Embracing Aging, Changing and Dying - Ram Dass (Riverhead Books-2000)

The Upside of Aging: How Long is Life Changing the World of Health, Work, Innovation, Policy and Purpose - Paul Irving (Wiley, 2014)

COACHING —

Becoming a Professional Life Coach: Lessons From the Institute of Life Coach Training- Patrick Williams and Diane S Menendez (W.W. Norton & Company-2007)

Coaching Questions - Tony Stoltzfus (www.coach22.com, 2008)

Invitation to Positive Psychology: Research and Tools for the Professional-Robert Biswas- Diener (Create Space   Independent Publishing, 2013)

Law & Ethics in Coaching : How to Solve and Avoid Difficult Problems In Your Practice- Patrick Williams & Sharon K. Anderson (John Wiley & Sons-2006)

Practicing Positive Psychology Coaching: Assessment, Activities and Strategies for Success - Robert Biswas-Diener (John Wiley & Sons, 2010)

Positive Psychology Coaching: Putting the Science of Happiness to Work for Your Clients- Robert Biswas-Diener and Ben Dean (John Wiley & Sons, 2007)

Total Life Coaching : A Compendium of Resources: 50+ Life Lessons, Skills, and Techniques to Enhance Your Practice...and Your Life - Patrick Williams and Lloyd J. Thomas (W. W. Norton & Company-2005)

COMPASSION —

Altruism: The Power of Compassion to Change Yourself and the World - Matthieu Ricard (Little Brown, 2015)

The Compassionate Mind: A New Approach to Life's Challenges - Paul Gilbert Ph.D. (New Harbinger Publications, 2009)

Empathy: Why it Matters and How to Get It - Roman Krznaric (Perigee Books, Penguin Group, 2014)

Give and Take: A revolutionary Approach to Success - Adam Grant (Penguin Books-2013)

How To Be Compassionate: Handbook for a Happier World - Dalai Lama

Self Compassion - Kristin Neff, PhD (HarperCollins Publishers, 2011)

The Selfish Society - Sue Gerhardt (Simon and Schuster-2011)

Twelve Steps to a Compassionate Life - Karen Armstrong (Anchor, 2010)

Why Kindness is Good For You - Dr David Hamilton (Hay House UK, 2010)

HAPPINESS —

The 10 Keys To Happier Living: A Practical Handbook for Happiness - Vanessa King, Action for Happiness (Headline Publishing Group, 2016)

The Art of Happiness at Work - Dalai Lama and Howard Cutler (Riverhead Books, 2013)

Being Happy: You Don't Have to be Perfect to Lead a Richer, Happier Life - Tal Ben-Shahar Ph.D. (McGraw-Hill, 2009)

Delivering Happiness:A Path to Profits, Passion and Purpose - Tony Hsieh (Writers of the Round Table Press, 2012)

The Geography of Bliss: One Grump's Search for the Happiest Places in the World - Eric Weiner (Hachette Book Group, 2008)

Great Days at Work: How Positive Psychology Can Transform Your Working Life - Suzanne Hazelton (Kogan Page Ltd, 2013)

Happiness: A Guide to Developing Life's Most Important Skill - Matthieu Ricard (Hachette Book Group, 2007)

Happiness: A History - Darrin M. McMahon (Atlantic Monthly Press, 2006)

The Happiness Advantage: The Seven Principles of Positive Psychology that Fuel Success and Performance at Work - Shawn Achor (Crown Publishing Group, 2010)

The Happiness Curve: Why Life Gets Better After 50 - Jonathan Rauch (St. Martin's Press, 2018)

Happiness by Design Finding Pleasure and Purpose in Everyday Life - Paul Dolan (Penguin Books, 2015)

Happiness: Lessons from a New Science - Richard Layard (Penguin Press, 2005)

Happiness: Unlocking the Mysteries of Psychological Wealth - Ed Diener and Robert Biswas-Diener Ph.Ds (Wiley-Blackwell, 2008)

The Happiness Hypothesis: Finding Modern Truth in Ancient Wisdom - Jonathan Haidt (Basic Books, 2006)

The Happy Manifesto: Make Your Organization a Great Workplace - Henry Stewart (Audible Studios, 2012)

The How of Happiness - Sonja Lyubomirisky (Penguin Press, 2008)

Love 2.0: Creating Happiness and Health in Moments of Connection - Barbara L. Fredrickson, Ph.D. (Hudson Street Press, 2013)

Mindset: The New Psychology of Success - Carol S. Dweck Ph.D. (Ballantine Books, 2016)

The Politics of Happiness: What Governments can Learn for the New Research on Well- Being - Derek Bok (Princeton University Press, 2010)

Stumbling on Happiness - Daniel Gilbert (Vintage Books, 2007)

World Happiness Report - Edited by John Helliwell, Richard Layard and Jeffrey Sachs

LEGACY —

Having The Last Say: Capturing Your Legacy in One Small Story - Alan Gelb (TarcherPerigee, 2015)

NEUROPLASTICITY —

The Brain That Changes Itself - Norman Doidge, MD (Penguin Books, 2007)

The Brain's Way of Healing: Remarkable Discoveries and Recoveries from the Frontiers of Neuroplasticity - Norman Doidge, MD (Viking Press, 2015)

Hardwiring Happiness: The New Brain Science of Contentment, Calm and Confidence -Rick Hanson, PhD (Harmony Books, 2013)

The Map of Heaven - Eben Alexander MD (Simon & Schuster, 2014)

Switch: How to Change Things When Change is Hard - Chip Heath and Dan Heath (Broadway Books, 2010)

The Way of Transition: Embracing Life's Most Difficult Moments - William Bridges (Da Capo Press, 2001)

PASSION —

The Boomerang Approach: Return to Purpose, Ignite your Passion - Reiner Lomb (Amazon Digital Services, 2014)

Jump Ship - Ditch your Dead End Job and Turn your Passion into a Profession - Josh Shipp (St. Martin's Press, 2013)

The Third Chapter: Passion, Risk and Adventure in the 25 Years After 50 - Sara Lawrence-Lightfoot (Sara Cricht on Books, 2009)

What's Next? Finding your Passion and Your Dream Job in your Forties, Fifties and Beyond - Kerry Hannon (Penguin Group, 2014)

PHILOSOPHY —

Change the World for a Fiver: We Are What We Do - anonymous author (Short Book Ltd, 2004)

Conversational Intelligence: How Great Leaders Build Trust and Get Extraordinary Results - Judith E. Glaser (Bibliomotion Inc., 2014)

Full Catastrophe Living - Jon Kabat-Zinn (Bantam Trade Books-2013)

How to Change the World - John Paul Flintoff (The School of Life, 2012)

How Much is Enough? Money and the Good Life - Robert and Edward Skidelsky (Other Press, 2013)

Philosophy for Life and Other Dangerous Situations - Jules Evans (New World Library, 2013)

The Power of Just Doing Stuff: How Local Action can Change the World - Rob Hopkins (Transition Books, 2013)

POSITIVE PSYCHOLOGY —

Authentic Happiness: Using the New Positive Psychology to Realize Your Potential for Lasting - Martin Seligman (Simon and Schuster, 2002)

Character Strengths and Virtues: A Handbook and Classification - Christopher Peterson, Martin E. P. Seligman (American Psychological Association, 2004)

Emotional Intelligence: Why it can Matter More than IQ - Daniel Goleman (Random House, 2005)

Flourish: A Visionary New Understanding of Happiness and Well Being - Martin Seligman (Free Press, 2011)

Flow: The Psychology of Optimal Experience - Mihaly Csikszent-mihalyi (First Harper, 1990)

Grit: The Power of Passion and Perseverance - Angela Duckworth, Ph.D. (Simon and Schuster, 2016)

Learned Optimism: How to Change Your Mind and Your Life - Martin Seligman (Vintage Books, 1990)

The Oxford Handbook of Positive Psychology - Shane J. Lopez, C.R. Snyder (Oxford Library of Psychology, 2009)

Positivity: Top-Notch Research Reveals the Upward Spiral That Will Change Your Life - Barbara Fredrickson (Three Rivers Press, 2009)

The Power of Positive Thinking - Norman Vincent Peale (Mandarin Paperbacks,1953)

Your Strengths Blueprint: How to be Engaged, Energized and Happy at Work - Michelle L McQuaid and Erin Lawns (Michelle McQuaid Pty Ltd, 2014)

PURPOSE —

Leading Well - The Essence of Wholehearted Inspirational Leaders - Randy Noe (CreateSpace, 2014)

Let Your Life Speak: Listening for the Voice of Vocation, Parker J. Palmer (Jossey-Bass, 1999)

Life Reimagined: Discovering your New Life Possibilities - Richard J. Leider and Alan M. Webber (Berrett-Koehler Publishers, 2013)

A New Purpose: Redefining Money, Family, Work, Retirement and Success, Ken Dychtwald Ph.D. and Daniel J Kadlec (Harper-Collins, 2010)

The Payoff Principle: Discover the 3 Secrets for Getting What You Want Out of Life and Work - Dr. Alan R. Zimmerman (Greenleaf Press, 2015)

The Power of Purpose: Find Meaning, Live Longer, Better - Richard J. Leider (Berrett-Koehler Publishers, 2015)

Sailing the Mystery: My Journey into Life's Remaining Chapters - Ed Merck (FriesenPress, 2013)

Second Wind: Navigating the Passage to a Slower, Deeper and more Connected Life - Dr. Bill Thomas (Simon and Schuster, 2014)

What Should I do with my Life? The True Story of People who

Answered the Ultimate Question - Po Bronson (Ballantine Books, 2005)

Your Life Calling: Reimagining the Rest of Your Life - Jane Pauley (Simon & Schuster, 2014)

REINVENTION AND SECOND ACTS —

Are You Old Enough to Read This Book: Reflections on Midlife - Readers Digest Association, 1997

The Big Leap: Conquer your Hidden Fear and Take Life to the Next Level - Gay Hendricks PhD (Harper One, 2009)

Boundless Potential - Mark S. Walton (McGraw Hill, 2012)

Catch Me Up: Your Best Days A re Not Behind You, The Future is Bright - William Shattner (Kickstarter, 2015)

Change Your Thinking, Change Your Life, How to Unlock Your Full Potential for Success and Achievement - Brian Tracy (John Wiley & Sons, 2003)

The Couple's Retirement Puzzle: 10 Must Have Conversations for Transitioning to the Second Half of Life - Roberta K Taylor and Dorian Mintzer (Lincoln Street Press, 2011)

The Creative Age: Awakening Human Potential in the Second Half of Life - Gene D. Cohen M.D., PhD. (Harper Collins, 2000)

Diary of a Company Man: Losing a Job, Finding a Life - James S Kunen (Lyons Press, 2012)

Do what you are. Discover the perfect career through the secrets of personality type - Paul D Tieger, Kelly Tieger, and Barbara Barron (Little Brown and Company, 5th Edition, 2014)

The Encore Career Handbook: How to Make a Living and a Difference in the Second Half of Life - Marci Alboher (Workman Publishing, 2013)

Happy Retirement: The Psychology of Reinvention - Professor Kenneth J Shultz, PhD. (Penguin Random House, 2015)

For My Next Act: Women Scripting Life After Fifty - Karen Baar (Rodale Books, 2004)

In Our Fifties: Voices of Men and Women Reinventing Their Lives - William H. Bergquist, Elinor Miller Greenberg, G and Alan Klaum (Sossey-Bass Publishers,1993)

In Our Prime: The Invention of Middle Age - Patricia Cohen (Scribner of Simon and Schuster Inc, 2012)

Is 65 the New 25? Reclaiming your Life; Becoming Who You were Meant to Be - Donna M Bennett (Travis Hornsby, 2015)

LEAP! What Will We Do with the Rest of our Lives? - Sara Davidson (Random House, 2007)

Live Smart After 50! - Natalie Eldridge (Life Planning Network Chairwoman, 2013).

Love Your Job: The New Rules for Career Happiness - Kerry Hannon (Wiley, 2015)

Mid-Life Magic: Designing the Next Chapter of Your Life - Lorraine Clemes, Ed.D (Amazon Digital Services, 2013)

The Pathfinder: How to Choose or Change your Career for a Lifetime of Satisfaction and Success - Nicholas Lore (Simon and Schuster, 1998)

Reinvention: How to Make the Rest of Your Life the Best of Your Life - Brian Tracy (Amacor Books, 2009)

Repurpose Your Career: A Practical Guide for Baby Boomers - Marc Miller with Susan Lahey (Career Pivot Publishing, 2013)

Second-Act Careers, 50+ Ways to Profit from your Passions During Semi-Retirement - Nancy Collamer, MS (Ten Speed Press, 2013)

Senior Wonders: People Who Achieved Their Dreams After Age 60 - Karen L. Pepkin & Wendell C.Taylor (Karrick Press, 2014)

Unretirement: How Baby Boomers are Changing the Way We Think about Work, Community and the Good Life - Chris Farrrell (Amazon Digital Services, 2014)

What Color is Your Parachute? 2014: A Practical Manual for Job Hunters and Career Changers - Richard Nelson Bolles (Ten Speed Press, 2013)

Work Reimagined: Uncover Your Calling - Richard J Leider and David A Shapiro (Life Reimagined.org, 2015)

RELATIONSHIPS —

Childhood and Society - Erik Erikson (Norton,1968)

Connected - Nicholas Christakis and James Fowler (Little Brown & Co, Hachette Books Group, 2009)

Dimensions of a New Identity -Erik Erikson (Jefferson lectures. W. W. Norton, 1973)

Games People Play: The Basic Handbook of Transactional Analysis - Eric Berne, MD (Ballantine Books, 1964)

Getting the Love You Want - Harville Hendrix Ph.D. (Henry Holt & Company, 1988)

The Gifts of Imperfection/Daring Greatly: Let go who you think you're supposed to be and embrace who you are - Brene Brown (Hazelden Publishing, 2010)

I'm OK You're OK: A practical Guide to Transactional Analysis - Thomas A. Harris MD (Harper and Row, 1967)

Motivation and Personality - Abraham Maslow **(**Harper Books, 1954**)**

People Skills - Robert Bolton Ph.D. (Prentice Hall Australia, 1987)

Please Understand Me: Character Temperament Types - David Keirsey and Marilyn Bates (Prometheus Nemesis Book Company, 1984)

Please Understand Me 2: Temperament, Character Intelligence - David Keirsey (Prometheus Nemesis Book Company, 1984)

Raising An Emotionally Intelligent Child: The Heart of Parenting - John Gottman PhD (Simon and Schuster, 1998)

The Relationship Cure - John Gottman Ph. D. (Three Rivers Press, 2001)

The Road to Character - David Brooks (Random House, 2015)

Theories of Personality - Duane P. Schultz & Sydney Ellen Schultz (Wadsworth, Cengage Learning, 2013)

Why Marriages Succeed or Fail and How You Can Make Yours Last - John Gottman, PhD (Simon and Schuster, 1994)

RESILIENCE —

Burn Out: The High Cost of High Achievement. What It is and How to Survive It - Freudenberger, Herbert and Richelson Géraldine (Bantam Books, 1980)

Courage: Formulas, Stories and Insights - Rabbi Zelig Pliskin (Artscroll, Shaar Press, 2000)

On Death and Dying - Elizabeth Kubler-Ross, MD (Scribner Books, 1968)

Reset - Kurt Andersen (Random House, 2009)

The Resilience Factor: 7 Keys to Finding Your Inner Strength and Overcoming Life's Hurdles - Karen Reivich and Andrew Shatte, Ph.D. (Broadway Books, 2003)

Resilient Grieving: Finding Strength and Embracing Life After a Loss That Changes Everything - Lucy Hone, Ph.D. (The Experiment LLC, 2017)

Willpower: Rediscovering the Greatest Human Strength - Roy F. Baumeister and John Tierney (Penguin Group, 2011)

WELL-BEING, SPIRITUALITY AND MIDLIFE —

Adult Personality: Toward a Psychology of Life Cycle, Middle Age and Aging - B L Neugarten (University of Chicago Press, 1968)

Awakening at Midlife - Kathleen Brehoney (Riverhead Books, 1996)

Being Mortal, Medicine and What Matters in the End - Atul Gawande (Metropolitan Books, 2014)

The Breaking Point: How Today's Women Are Navigating Midlife Crisis - Sue Shellenberger (Holt Paperbacks, 2005)

Death of a Hero, Birth of the Soul - J C Robinson (Council Oaks Books,1995)

Falling Upward: A Spirituality for the Two Halves of Life - Father Richard Rohr (Wiley, 2011)

Human Being: A Manual for Happiness, Health, Love and Wealth - Dave Ellis and Stan Lankowitz (Breathrough Enterprises, 1995)

Life Reimagined: The Science, Art and Opportunity of Midlife - Barbara Bradley Hagerty (Riverhead Books, 2016)

Man's Search for Meaning - Viktor E. Frankl (Beacon Press, 2006)

Mindfulness: A Practical Guide to Finding Peace in a Frantic World - Professor Mark Williams and Dr. Danny Penman (Little Brown Books, 2011)

Modern Man in Search of a Soul - Carl Jung (Harcourt Brace, 1933)

Not For Sale: Finding Center in the Land of Crazy Horse - Kevin Hancock (Seventh Power Press, 2015)

Organizational Sleepwalkers: Emotion Distress at Midlife - Manfred Kets de Vries (Wiley, 1999)

Portfolio Life: The New Path to Work, Purpose and Passion After 50 - David Corbett, Richard Higgins (Josey Bass, 2006)

The Seasons of Man's Life - D J Levinson, C N Darrow, DB Klein, M H Levinson and B McKee (Ballantine Books, 1978)

The Science of Well Being - Felicia A. Huppert, Nick Baylis, Barry Keverne (Oxford University Press, 2007)

Not For Sale: Finding Center in the Land of Crazy Horse - Kevin Hancock (Seventh Power Press, 2015)

ABOUT THE AUTHOR

"Being listened to is so much like love that you cannot tell the difference." -
David Oxberg

Dr. Andrew S. Kane, OBE, Ph.D. has experienced the heights of professional, personal, and academic success yet also suffered the devasta-
tion of loss, most notably that of his 27-year-old daughter in 2008.
Nothing can sharpen the thrill of success by having experienced
defeat. By developing his own coping skills and building his resilience,
he has bounced back from multiple losses of family, friends, and
Arthur Andersen, to name but a few.

These experiences have permitted Dr. Kane to witness his journey
through adulthood and to write about it using his knowledge and
experience including those from his professional and academic
pursuits.

Today, he positively impacts people at all stages of transitioning
through adulthood by sharpening their decision making, developing
their relationship, emotional intelligence, and resilience skills to enable
them to be better people, achieve better results, and enhance their wellbeing in order to positively impact their employees, families, and
communities. He touches the heart of many by helping people address
the issues that impact their heart and tear at their gut such as deep
losses or life events by addressing midlife challenges, fears, and
conflicts in understanding and working with younger generations such
as Gen Z and Millennials.

Over the past few decades, he has honed his own skills through
managing single family offices for wealthy families, been CEO of
HSBC Private Bank in Southern California and was a Managing

Partner at Arthur Andersen for 30 years. He has also served on over 25 boards for profit and not-for-profit organizations, some pubic and some private. He is also Chairman of a family-owned retail business based in San Francisco.

Academically, Dr. Kane has a Ph.D. (Doctorate) and Master's degrees in Human Development and Professional Coaching from the International University of Professional Studies (IUPS) and he is also a graduate of the London School of Economics. He also serves on the faculty of the International University of Professional Studies.

Professionally, he is a Fellow Chartered Accountant (FCA) of The Institute of Chartered Accountants in England and Wales and a Member of both the American and California Institutes of Certified Public Accountants (CPA). However, in both countries he no longer is in practice.

He is a Member of the International Coaching Federation (ICF), the Harvard Institute of Coaching (IOC) and last, but not least, the International Positive Psychology Association (IPPA) as he is a globally certified positive psychology coach.

About twenty years ago, Dr. Kane was invested by Her Majesty The Queen as an Officer of the British Empire (OBE) for his services to U.S. and UK business relationships. Apart from being the author of "Three Bridges - Adulthood Is Easy Until Life Intervenes," he authored "Addressing Midlife" as his Ph.D. doctoral thesis and has authored or co-authored numerous articles and spoken frequently on radio, TV, and at conferences.

He is a citizen of both the UK and USA. He and his wife live on an island in Westlake Village. Their family, however, is spread across the globe from Bali, Indonesia, across the USA, and in the United Kingdom, so travel and spending time with friends and family is a constant in their lives.

You can learn more about Dr. Kane and his work here:
https://www.andrewskane.com/
or via LinkedIn:
https://www.linkedin.com/in/andrewskane/

Made in the USA
San Bernardino, CA
23 November 2018